BLISSFUL STATE OF SURRENDER

BLISSFUL STATE OF SURRENDER

SANITA FEJZIĆ

PLAYWRIGHTS CANADA PRESS
TORONTO

First edition: February 2025
Printed and bound in Canada by Imprimerie Gauvin Ltée, Gatineau

Jacket art by Salini Perera

Playwrights Canada Press
202-269 Richmond St. W., Toronto, ON M5V 1X1
416.703.0013 | info@playwrightscanada.com | www.playwrightscanada.com

LIBRARY AND ARCHIVES CANADA CATALOGUING IN PUBLICATION
Title: Blissful state of surrender / Sanita Fejzić.
Names: Fejzić, Sanita, 1985- author.
Description: First edition. | In English, with some text in Bosnian with English translation.
Identifiers: Canadiana (print) 20240514912 | Canadiana (ebook) 20240523806 | ISBN 9780369105332 (softcover) | ISBN 9780369105356 (EPUB) | ISBN 9780369105349 (PDF)
Subjects: LCGFT: Drama.
Classification: LCC PS8611.E455 B55 2025 | DDC C812/.6—dc23

Playwrights Canada Press staff work across Turtle Island, on Treaty 13 and Treaty 20 territories, as well as unceded lands, which are the current, ancestral, and future homes of the Anishinaabe Nations (Ojibwe / Chippewa, Odawa, Potawatomi, Algonquin, Saulteaux, Nipissing, and Mississauga / Michi Saagiig), the Wendat, members of the Haudenosaunee Confederacy (Mohawk, Oneida, Onondaga, Cayuga, Seneca, and Tuscarora), and the xʷməθkʷəy̓əm (Musqueam), Sḵwx̱wú7mesh (Squamish), and səlilwətaɬ (Tsleil-Waututh) Nations, as well as Metis and Inuit peoples. It always was and always will be Indigenous land.

We acknowledge the financial support of the Canada Council for the Arts, the Ontario Arts Council (OAC), Ontario Creates, the Government of Ontario, and the Government of Canada for our publishing activities.

Canada Council for the Arts | Conseil des arts du Canada
ONTARIO ARTS COUNCIL
CONSEIL DES ARTS DE L'ONTARIO
an Ontario government agency
un organisme du gouvernement de l'Ontario
ONTARIO CREATES | ONTARIO CRÉATIF
Canada
Ontario

To Fikreta and Muzafer Fejzić

FOREWORD

SUAD BUSHNAQ

It was my absolute honour to be the music composer for Sanita Fejzić's incredible and important play, *Blissful State of Surrender*. As a Canadian of partly Bosniak origin (my surname, Bushnaq, literally means Bosniak), working on a Bosnian Canadian project was a dream come true. It was an honour and a privilege, as well as a huge responsibility. I wanted to make sure that my music, while acting as a grounding "glue" in the play and giving it a unique sonic identity, had a blend of cinematic elements and traditional Bosnian elements. As someone who's listened to a lot of Bosnian music during her life, the musical language of Sevdalinkas was in my genes. I wanted to incorporate this tradition, while making it unique to this very unique story.

During my twenty years of life in Canada, I have witnessed first-hand the blatant Islamophobia which was rampant post 9/11, and how people saw–and still see–us, Muslims of all backgrounds, as one monolithic group. The dehumanization and "othering" of Muslims continues to happen today, sometimes resulting in internalized Islamophobia amongst Muslims who are trying to "fit in." For me, Sanita's play offers an important insight into the daily lives of a Muslim family with all the diverse colours that make it what it is: a European Muslim family forcibly displaced from its original home, trying to adapt to Canadian society in different ways based on each individual's own definition and idea of what makes a Bosnian a Bosnian, a Muslim a Muslim, and a Canadian a Canadian. There was something extremely refreshing in the multilayered characters

Sanita created, which provide valuable insight into the uniqueness of Bosnian identity, and something extremely fascinating in the complex, yet very relatable, family dynamics she created. I myself remember similar conflicts arising in my own family as someone who is part Bosnian, part Syrian, part Palestinian and it was important for me to reflect this diversity, conflict, and also the beauty of all these contrasting colours in the music I created for *Blissful State of Surrender*.

I wanted to hire live musicians currently living in Sarajevo, and was lucky to get the amazing accordionist Adis Sirbubalo and the wonderful clarinetist Meho Radoović on board, both of whom provided priceless authenticity in the performance of the melodies I composed. To get the "sound" of Sarajevo in their recordings—to be able to hear the air in a room in Sarajevo in the recordings—and to incorporate these recordings into the rest of the music textures, was a breathtaking experience for me. My entire career as a music composer stems from the fact that I have generational trauma due to genocides committed against my ancestors on all sides of my genetic makeup. The only place I can truly call home is my music, where I can express myself, with all the complexities of my being, in one place, with no judgement. Being able to translate trauma, displacement, identity, family, and the essence of what it means to be European and Muslim at the same time through writing the original music score for a play as powerful as *Blissful State of Surrender* was not only a job I had to do, nor just an artistic collaboration: it was a personal healing journey. I want to thank Sanita for entrusting me with creating the musical world for her immensely important play, and for giving me a once in a lifetime chance to experience what it's like to be a Bosnian Canadian through my music.

Hailed as an "incredible artist" by Hans Zimmer, Suad Bushnaq is an internationally acclaimed, multi-award winning Jordanian Canadian music composer of Bosnian, Palestinian, and Syrian roots. Her work has garnered a CASMA (Canadian Screen Music Award), a Hollywood Music in Media Award, and four CSA (Canadian Screen Award) nominations, to name a few. She is the 2021 recipient of the Kathleen McMorrow Music

Award from the Ontario Arts Foundation. Her most recent work includes the three-part series Secret World of Sound with David Attenborough, *for which she won a Canadian Screen Music Award and was nominated for a Hollywood Music in Media Award.*

FOREWORD

KEITH BARKER

Blissful State of Surrender first came to me by way of actor John Koensgen. John had recently been cast in a small production of the play at the Great Canadian Theatre Company and was deeply moved by the piece. John wrote that he felt compelled to reach out about this brilliant new work, one that he believed deserved a bigger life. I immediately reached out to Sanita and requested the script—I've learned that when an artist of John's calibre speaks so highly of a play, it is wise to take notice.

The play was everything John promised it would be. *Blissful State of Surrender* reflected Sanita's lived experience, portraying a Bosnian Muslim family's journey across three countries, going from illegal immigrant to a "temporary guest" to finding permanent refuge in Canada after being forced to flee the Siege of Sarajevo and the genocide of the Bosniak people. In the hands of a less talented writer this play might succumb to the heaviness of the subject matter, but Sanita's brilliant and thoughtful use of comedy allows audiences to engage with the difficult subject matter.

Comedy doesn't erase trauma, but it can provide a way in. It allows us to approach sensitive material with a sense of shared humanity, making it easier to reflect on and process. Laughter is a release, a connector that helps us to hold the weight of a difficult story without feeling overwhelmed by it.

At its core, *Blissful State of Surrender* asks us what it means to call a place—or a person—home. Through the lens of a family living in the shadows of a war that displaced them, Sanita explores the sacrifices people make for their family, the silence that trauma often imposes, and the love and resilience that carries us forward. Sanita's characters are richly complex, reminding us that all of humanity has more in common with each other than we have differences that divide us. Blending English and Bosnian seamlessly, the play draws together the world this family finds themselves in with the world they had to flee, creating moments that puncture the heart. I didn't always understand what was being said, but the emotions of the moment transcended borders, histories, and language. I felt every word.

There has been some fascinating research about how audiences' heartbeats become synced during a live performance. It's a beautiful metaphor for what happens in such a room, especially for stories like this. Theatres don't just remind us that we are not alone; it allows us to feel it, physically and emotionally, in real time. For plays that navigate the dark but show us the light, that coherence is especially vital. It's not about erasing the pain but, rather, holding it together in a way that transforms it.

Blissful State of Surrender is a rare gift, told with a big heart and a deft hand. In a world that sometimes feels too small to contain our hopes for a shared future within our collective histories, this play reminds us that within everyone's story lies a bit of our own.

Keith Barker is a Métis artist from Northwestern Ontario. He is the director of the Foerster Bernstein New Play Development Program at the Stratford Festival and the former artistic director at Native Earth Performing Arts in Toronto. In 2023 Keith was a recipient of the Johanna Metcalf Performing Arts Prize, and in 2020 he received a Dora Mavor Award for Outstanding New Play as well as the Playwrights Guild of Canada's Carol Bolt Award. Keith was a finalist for the Governor General's Literary Award for Drama in 2018 for his play, This Is How We Got Here. *He received a Saskatchewan and Area Theatre Award for Achievement in Playwriting for his play* The Hours That Remain, *as well as a Yukon Arts Award for Best Art for Social Change. Keith returned to the stage in 2023, playing Louis Riel in France Koncan's* Women of the Fur Trade *for the Stratford Festival. Other acting credits include Richard Hannay in Bruce County Playhouse's* The 39 Steps, *Cornwall in the National Arts Centre's production of* King Lear, *Roger Hughes in* Seeds, *and Bernard Smoke in* Fury *at the Blyth Festival.*

AUTHOR'S PREFACE

In writing *Blissful State of Surrender*, I have tried my best to approximate a realistic portrait of the Bosnian refugee-immigrant experience. The play attempts to translate things that cannot be spoken—to show the ghosts that haunt every survivor of the 1992–1995 Balkan War and genocide of my Muslim Bosniak people.

To translate that which is beyond words is to stage the lived poetry of complex human experiences. Bosnian immigrants have a particular way of speaking that goes beyond the Slavic accent and echoes its unique warring, lamented, joyful and generous everyday poetics. The Bosnian refugee-immigrant's imagination is as deep and complex as is their troubled history. From the medieval Bosnian state to the Ottoman rule, the Austro-Hungarian occupation, the Kingdom of Yugoslavia, World War II, Tito's Socialist Federal Republic of Yugoslavia, and the 1992–1995 war and genocide, Bosnians are scarred with beautiful and striking—even if deeply hurt—collisions with the past.

This play was written in honour of Šuhra Fejzić, *moja rahmetli nena*, my devotedly Muslim grandmother brutally murdered during the genocide. It is dedicated to the approximately 100,000 Bosnians killed, of whom 80% were Muslim Bosniaks. It remembers the approximately 12,000 to 50,000 Bosniak women and girls raped during the genocide, and their children. Finally, it was written for the 2.2 million Muslim, Catholic, and Orthodox Bosnians who were forced into exile during the genocide, the largest exodus in Europe since World War II. The loss of connection to culture and country, and our mother tongue, remains a continued source of unrest and pain. May *Blissful State of Surrender* bring love, healing, and hope for a world without war, genocide, and other forms of organized violence.

Blissful State of Surrender was first produced at the Great Canadian Theatre Company, Ottawa, on February 22, 2022, with the following cast and creative team:

Anurag Choudhury: Jidu
John Koensgen: Emir
Andrea Massoud: Senka
Danielle Savoie: Agata
Kate Smith: Maja
Zvjezdana (Dana) Užarević: Suzana

Suad Bushnaq: Composer
Laurie Champagne: Stage Manager
Sanita Fejzić: Playwright & Producer
Jennifer Goodman: Set & Lighting Designer
Vanessa Imeson: Costume Designer
Venessa Lachance: Sound Designer
Jamaal Jackson Rogers: Cultural Consultant
Laurie Shannon: Production Manager
Bronwyn Steinberg: Director
Arielle Voght: Assistant Stage Manager

NOTES

Sue and Emir speak in a thick Bosnian accent. Their spoken English employs Bosnian syntax, which is why, for example, the position of subject and verb is reversed.

Intimate scenes involving the parents are spoken in Bosnian. The rest of the family also sometimes speaks in Bosnian and German. English translations are provided within square brackets immediately following lines in Bosnian and German.

The action takes place during a stormy winter evening in the suburb of a Canadian city. The location, and related lines, can be changed to other countries with permission from the playwright.

CHARACTERS

Suzana Bolić (nicknamed Sue and Suzo), mother.
Emir Bolić, father.
Maja Bolić (pronounced Maya), eldest daughter.
Senka Bolić, second daughter.
Agata Bolić, youngest daughter.
Jidu Hebbar, Maja's friend.

ACT 1

Large open space living and dining room area, including a dining room table upon which sits an extravagant, fuchsia pink bowl. There is also a fireplace, a couch and two chairs, and a large arched floor lamp. SUE *stands by the dining room table, opening a bottle of red.* EMIR *enters carrying a canvas.*

EMIR: *Suzo, ajde pomozi mi.* Come on, *ženo*! *Hajde bona!* [Suzo, come help me! Come on!]

SUE: Hey, hey, *čovječe—polako*! *Čistim kuću cijeli dan, zar ne vidiš? Joj, Bože! Jel' boja svježa?* My chair! [Hey, hey—slow down. I've been cleaning the house all day long, can't you see? Oh, God! Is that paint fresh? My chair!]

EMIR: *Ha? Šta misliš? Sve su boje koje si tražila:* "midnight black" and "sandy beige." [What do you think? It's all the colours you asked for: "midnight black" and "sandy beige."]

SUE: *Pa nije loše, ljubavi. Nego . . .* [It's not bad, darling. But . . .] whose face is that? *Ko je to?* [Who is she?]

EMIR: *Zar nevidiš da si ti?* [Can't you tell it's you?]

SUE: *Kako, bolan? Uopšte ne liči na mene.* [How is that possible? She doesn't look anything like me.]

EMIR: *Ti, kad si bila mlada i manje kritična.* [You, when you were younger and less critical.]

SUE: *Ma molim te, Emir!* [Please, Emir!] When it was the last time you look at my body, anyway? *To je assistant od tvog šefa. Kako se zove žena? Alicia. Slikaš mi svoju ljubavnicu. Jel' moguće? Bože moj!* [This is your boss's assistant. What's the woman's name? Alicia. You've painted your mistress and given it to me. What audacity! Dear God!]

EMIR: Alicia? *Suzo, bona, dosta je tvoje ljubomore!* [Suzo, I've had enough of your jealousy!] And don't talk so loud, Agata gonna hear you.

SUE: Agata can't hear us—she married to her headphones.

EMIR: *Ajde bona* [Come on]: control yourself . . . and, and put that bottle away, *molim te* [please].

EMIR picks up the painting.

Stavit ću je iznad kamina. [I'm nailing it above the fireplace.]

SUE: Not above the fireplace! *Nema šanse, Emire. Ovo je naša kuća, i kažem ti da je nećeš staviti gdje ja jedem i pijem.* [No way, Emir. This is our house, and I'm telling you that you will not hang this where I eat and drink.]

EMIR: *Šta? Ma bona ženo,* [What? Come on, woman] don't play tricks with me! *Naša kuća? Naša kuća? Čija je ova lampa? Specifično sam ti rekao da je ne kupiš!* [Our house? Our house? Whose lamp is this? I specifically asked you not to buy it!]

SUE: *Šta je s tom lampom, ha?* [What's wrong with the lamp, huh?]

EMIR: This lamp is piece of shit! *Kakva je to lampa koja ne osvijetli cijelu sobu? Što si je kupila? I ovu sofu, huh?* [What kind of a lamps doesn't light up a whole room? Why did you even buy it? And what about this sofa, huh?]

SUE: *Ah, ne, Emire! Kupili smo ovu sofu zajedno.* [Oh, no Emir! We bought this sofa together.]

EMIR: *Zajedno? Ko bona? Ti i moja Mastercard?* [Together? Who? You and my Mastercard?]

SUE: *Jel' se ti to pretvaraš?* [Are you joking?]

EMIR: I don't remember!

SUE: *Normalno, bolan! Nigdje me ne vodiš, osim u Loblaws ili Walmart—ne vjeruješ da mogu kupiti pravi jogurt.* [Of course! You don't take me anywhere except Loblaws or Walmart—you don't trust I'll buy the right kind of yogurt.]

EMIR: *Hoću* Activia plain *yogurt! Jel to previse za tebe?* [I want Activia plain yogurt! Is that too much to ask of you?]

SUE: *Ma pusti me na miru, Emire. Idi sam u šoping onda!* [Leave me be, Emir. Go shopping on your own then!]

EMIR: *Hoćeš da idem u šoping sa tobom da te gledam dok kupuješ ovakve grozne floroscentno ružičaste zdjele sa mojim parama?* [You want me to go shopping with you so I can watch you buy horrible fluorescent pink bowls with my money?]

EMIR picks up the bowl.

SUE: *I šta ćeš sada, jeli?* [What are you going to do now, tell me?]

Tense silence.

EMIR: Nothing, *ženo moja* [dear wife], what do you want from me? I try make you happy, you not happy. Always same story.

SUE hits her head on the lamp.

SUE: *Ma jebem ti!* [Damn it!]

EMIR: You see? What I tell you?

There is a knock on the door.

EMIR: I know that knock. It's Senka!

SUE: Agata! Come down, darling. Party is starting now!

EMIR opens the door. SENKA enters.

SENKA: *Tata!* [Dad!] How are you?

EMIR: My darling, Senka, I good, how are you? Quick, quick, come in. *U pičku materinu!* [Swears in Bosnian] That's a hell of a snowfall.

SENKA: They're saying fifty centimetres by tomorrow morning.

SUE: Come in, come in, *ljubavi* [my love].

EMIR: Here, let me take your stuff. *(beat)* I going out for quick smoke. Bye!

EMIR exits.

SENKA: I thought he quit smoking.

SUE: He did. He does, every year. Your father is professional quitter.

SENKA: Quitting's tough.

SUE serves wine.

Oh! Nice new fruit bowl. Very pink.

SUE: Thank you! Twenty dollars at Winners, can you believe it?

They toast.

SENKA: To you and Tata! And to Agata! Where is she?

SUE: I don't know what's wrong with her. Lately, she avoid me or treat me like complete stranger.

SENKA: She's ready to leave the house. Maybe she needs some space?

SUE: What you are talking about, Senka? She just a child.

SENKA: She turns twenty today.

SUE: Exactly.

SENKA: Okay. Let's not argue. I've had a long day.

SUE: Argue, who arguing here? Your sister stay locked up in her room on that computer all day. Just like your father. If he's not at work, he in the basement watching TV.

SENKA: Mama! You tell me this every time we see each other.

SUE: And nothing changes. Nothing. Your father doesn't notice me. Maja never calls back. And you! Since you started that Ph.D., you too busy to see your own mother.

SENKA: Mama! I'm not in the mood for this—this negativity.

SENKA checks her phone.

SUE: This not negativity, this just life, *Senko moja* [my Senka].

SENKA: It's always the same story. It drives me crazy! *Ich kann es nicht mehr ertragen.* [German: I can't stand it anymore.]

SUE: *Ich bin nicht verrückt!* [German: I'm not crazy!] Don't talk to your mother like that.

SENKA: Did I say *you* were crazy?

SUE: You see how hard my life is? All I do is cook and clean. Nobody appreciate me.

SENKA: How much food did you make?

SUE: Not much. These just appetizers. For dinner, I have *sarma, pita krompiruša*, Agata's favourite, and some *ćevapčići* for your father. I also make some chicken and rice, and a few other things.

SENKA: I thought it was just the five of us.

SUE: Why you keep texting in the middle of conversation?

SENKA: Ahmet is on his way as we speak, making a connection through New York. In this weather . . . God.

SUE: You just like me—you gonna marry a man who's never around. It's lonely to have absent husband.

SENKA: He visits once a month! *(beat)* Is that how you feel, Mama? Are *you* lonely?

SUE: Lonely? Forget lonely, *Senko moja*—I am invisible. Look at me, *sine* [child], look at me! I take good care of myself. And you know what? Your father barely see me.

> *SUE runs to the window. She hides behind the curtain, obviously spying on EMIR.*

SENKA: For God's sake, Mama!

SUE: You no care! You just like *him*. Same blood, same temperament! You don't even care that your fiancé is dreaming of Canadian passport!

SENKA: Excuse me? Ahmet could immigrate here in a split second and you know it! He's a skilled worker! Ugh!

SUE: Oh, Allah. What have I done for my whole family to treat me this way?

SENKA: You have this pattern of saying the same thing over and over again. It's like a slow-acting venom. After a while, it seeps in and poisons everything.

SUE: *(points to painting)* Your father cheating on me with woman from his work. Look at his latest masterpiece! She younger than you. He talking to her on the cell phone right now. Outside! In minus twenty conditions. Can you believe it?

SENKA: I can't talk to you anymore. I'm gonna go see Agata.

SENKA exits.

SUE: Just like your father. Walk away! *Mrš.* [Get lost!] Oh, my kids torture me but here comes the real reason for my headache.

EMIR enters.

EMIR: *Suzo moja!* [My Sue!] Where is Senka? And Agata? Agata! *Senko*! Senka! This is going to be the best party! Good thing you made me dress up! Good thing you overcooked!

SUE: What are you talking about, *bolan*?

EMIR: I have feeling you going to be happy! I so happy! Open the bottle of rakija, *bona*!

SUE: Is that how cigarette make you feel?

EMIR: Yes! Cigarette makes me feel wonderful! Amazing! I looking forward to next one already.

SUE: Your daughter engaged to man we barely know and all you do is smoke!

EMIR: She gonna marry who she wants, I don't care.

SUE: What kind of a man is named Ahmet Ahmetić?

EMIR: So? Better than your uncle, Islam Hadži-hafiz-begović—longest name on earth.

EMIR looks at his watch.

SUE: *Čuj, bože.* [Listen to him, God.] You making fun of my eighty-year-old uncle from small village in Bosnia?

EMIR: You making fun of our daughter's fiancé from slightly bigger village in Bosnia.

SUE: What if she get pregnant and no finish her PH.D.?

EMIR: You crazy? She my daughter, she no stupid. That's enough talking about silly things.

SUE: What silly things? Why you keep looking at your watch?

EMIR: I'm happy, *ženo*! This is going to be a day you won't forget, *trust me*.

SUE: How can I forget, Emir? Ahmet Ahmetić. Ahmet Ahmetić, *bolan*!

EMIR: What you keep saying his name? You sound like broken record.

SUE: Exactly.

EMIR: Look, he ask me if he can marry her. I say yes. What you want now?

SUE: Why you say yes without talking to your wife, hah?

EMIR: If Senka say yes to him, then that's it. What's gonna happen if I say no, hah? She gonna turn her back on us, like Maja.

SUE: Of course, of course, we no want that. But—

EMIR: No but—that's it!

EMIR slams the table.

SUE: I no trust him, Emir.

EMIR: Ahmet very nice guy, smart businessman.

SUE: He working for shady Saudi Arabian real estate firm. My cousin Sajra tell me.

EMIR: So what, huh? Europe, Canada, America—they watch us die on TV! If it was not for Saudi Arabia sending money and men during the war, we all be dead. Now Saudi Arabia helping young Bosnian men get jobs, *pah*!

SUE: You a man—you don't understand. Listen to me: Senka may gonna have to wear hijab!

EMIR laughs.

You stupid man. You have no idea what it's like to be woman in this world.

EMIR: I give you $100 if Senka wear hijab even for one day.

SUE shakes her head.

What's problem here, Suzo? Your mother wear hijab.

SUE: It's not hijab. It's head scarf, *šamija*. For older women—nobody is forcing them!

EMIR: My sister-in-law is forty and she wear hijab. Sarajevo change after the war. The women more Muslim than before.

SUE: Now women wear niqab in downtown Baščaršija. Can you believe it?

EMIR: Maybe Senka right . . .

Beat

You have internalize Islamophobia!

SUE: What you talking about?

EMIR: I don't know—ask your daughter!

SUE: This not about me, *bolan*. Watch what gonna happen when she marry Ahmet Ahmetić.

EMIR: Okay, Suzo. She wear niqab, go to Mosque like good Muslim girl, and give up her career. Finally, at least one woman in this house gonna become domesticate!

SUE: Is no joke, Emir. Because of his job, Ahmet speak Arabic more than Bosnian!

EMIR: So what? Bosnian full of Arabic words I proud to speak. What you say to your brother when you call him?

Silence.

You say *merhaba* and *aleikum selam*. And what you say when Iman's daughter have baby?

SUE: I no remember!

EMIR: *Elhamdulila! Mašalah!*

SUE: Of course, her first baby just born!

EMIR: So what the problem if Senka's children speak better Arabic than you and me, hah? Let Senka go where life take her. When she marry man, she must follow him. That's it—end of story!

SUE: You no listening to me—

EMIR: You right! So why you still talking?

The doorbell rings.

She's home! You're home! Maja, welcome, welcome.

SUE: Oh my God. Allah has answered my prayers!

MAJA: Tata, it's so good to see you!

EMIR: *(yelling)* Come, jewels of my life, come say hi to Maja. She's home!

SUE: My love, my heart!

MAJA: *Mama! Kako si bona? Što plačeš?* [How are you? Why are you crying?] Why are you crying?

SUE: My light. I crying because I so happy to see you, *sine*.

MAJA: I'm happy to see you too, *Majkice* [Mom].

SUE: You lost weight, *ljubavi*. You look so pale, Maja. Are you eating?

MAJA: I'm fine, Mama.

SUE: *Jesili umorna, sine? Jesili došla direktno iz Vankuver?* [Are you tired, darling? Was it a direct flight from Vancouver?]

MAJA: *Da, Majko. Evo stigla ima četres pet minuta.* [Yes, Mom. The flight landed forty-five minutes ago.]

SUE: Is that really you, *moja majka* [my mother]?

EMIR: God, you look different.

MAJA: Yes, it's really me.

EMIR: You look the same.

SUE: *Ljubavi mamina.* [My love.]

SENKA: Maja! Look who finally decided to treat us with her presence.

MAJA: Senka!

SENKA: Good to see you. You here for Gata's birthday?

MAJA: How could I miss it? Where is Gata? Have you all *(beat)* spoken?

SENKA: Not yet. She's upstairs. Refusing to open the door.

MAJA: How are you? Congrats on the engagement. *(beat)* Sorry I couldn't make it to the party . . .

SENKA: Right. But you *are* here for Gata's birthday.

SUE: *Ma hajmo, ljubavi moje.* [Come on, my loves.] You sisters—you were like twins growing up. You have to love each other, no fighting.

MAJA: What's up with her?

SUE: She just cranky because her fiancé live on other side of the planet.

MAJA & SENKA: Mama!

SUE: We only seen him twice, once when he ask Emir if he can marry our daughter! Can you believe it?

SENKA: Seriously? He's here once a month! C'mon! Mom's just having problems with Tata.

SENKA texts on her phone.

EMIR: Problem with me? Leave me out of it.

SUE: Leave you out of it? Who you were talking to on phone just now? You think I no see you?

EMIR laughs.

You find that funny? That sad, not funny, *bolan*.

MAJA: He was talking to me. Well, actually Jidu. You remember Jidu? Jidu Hebbar?

SUE: Of course, I remember Jidu! He the boy with long hair. Your high school sweetheart.

MAJA: No. We never um, ugh—anyway, he picked me up at the airport so I could surprise you! Zero visibility on the road! Tata helped with directions.

SUE: That take, what, five minutes? You were on phone almost fifteen!

EMIR hits his head on the lamp on his way to sit on the couch.

EMIR: Goddamn lamp. Goddamn no peace in this house.

He picks up a magazine and pretends to read it.

SUE: No, you cannot get away with this, Emir. I saying it in front of girls. You having an affair with that woman from Barbados, Alicia. Shame on you! She could be your daughter!

EMIR: You just jealous because I'm attractive man.

EMIR dramatically brings the magazine to his face.

SUE: I see you smirk! I call Maja, tell her I gonna divorce you. This why she come home.

MAJA: Oh, Mama. Tsk!

SUE: Of course that's why you come, *sine*! Why else you here?

MAJA: I just want to be here for Gata, you know? God! I'm dehydrated.

SUE: Have some wine, *ljubavi*.

MAJA: No, thanks.

SUE: Is from Montenegro!

MAJA: No, thanks, Mama. Not for me.

SUE: And you, don't flatter yourself. You not as good looking as you think.

The doorbell rings. SUE opens the door.

JIDU enters with MAJA's luggage, a guitar strapped to his back.

SUE: Oh my God! Jidu!

JIDU: Wow—Sue! How are you?

SUE: I good and you?

JIDU: Excellent, thank you.

SUE: Why you wearing guitar instead of jacket? It's snowstorm outside!

JIDU: I thought it'd be nice. *(beat)* Gosh, it's been—what—over a decade? You look the same: stunning!

SUE: Well, I don't know about that. I carry four children, getting old now.

SENKA: *Four* children, Mama? Four? You should probably relax with that Montenegro wine of yours.

SUE: Well—who's counting? And please, *Senko*, you not here to babysit me. I have no problems with my wine, thank you very much, I *very* relaxed already.

MAJA: Thanks for the luggage, Jidu.

EMIR walks over.

JIDU: No problem.

MAJA: Well. I'll call you later?

JIDU: Oh . . . of course.

EMIR: Thank you for driving my daughter. It was good to see you.

They shake hands. EMIR opens the front door.

Okay. Goodbye now. Goodbye—*hajde* [let's go].

SUE closes door.

SUE: What you are doing? Where are your manners? Jidu, please, come in, come in. Sit down. We having a birthday party. You remember Agata? She turning twenty today.

JIDU: Thanks, Sue. Happy to stay. Hey—Senka. Wow, you're a grown woman.

SENKA does not lift her face off the phone.

SENKA: Hey, Jidu. Good to see you.

JIDU: Heard you were getting married. Congrats!

SENKA: Thanks!

Pause.

JIDU: You guys renovated. Nice bowl! And, wow, look at that painting!

EMIR: Thank you! *(yelling)* Agata! Come down now or we start the party without you! Maja is here! Jidu also here. Don't be rude.

SUE: Why you so loud? *(to MAJA)* I wish you tell me you gonna come. I would have invited our friends and family, and the neighbours.

MAJA: Thank God I didn't! I wouldn't have liked that at all.

JIDU: She gets super nervous in group settings.

EMIR: Sit down everyone, take a seat. You too, Senka, get off couch and say proper hello to your sister—*please.*

SENKA hugs her sister. There is a visible discomfort between them.

SENKA: Good to see you.

MAJA: You too lil' sis.

Silence.

Oh, *Senko* . . . let's not . . . I just got here . . . *(beat)* I'm here for Agata's birthday. She emailed me . . .

SENKA: Okay. *(beat)* Well, I'm glad someone has succeeded in getting you to come home. Take some time to settle in before the Bosnian drama begins.

MAJA: Thanks, I guess.

SENKA: I have to call Ahmet, excuse me.

SENKA exits. Everyone sits around the table. SUE serves drinks.

SUE: I love your sweater, Jidu.

JIDU: Thanks, I got it at the Salvation Army for a dollar.

SUE: Oh?

EMIR: Ha! Ask her how much that dress cost.

SUE: Forgive my husband, he always in bad mood.

EMIR: Someone is in bad mood? Not me! I'm fine.

JIDU: Ah, I've missed you guys. Really. It's nice to be here again.

SUE: Maja, sweetheart, what a surprise. I still in shock. I can't believe you really here.

EMIR: Yeah, yeah, ignore me. I like beer better anyway. Water is for washing feet, beer is for drinking.

SUE: Emir, please.

The audience hears SENKA *from the kitchen.*

SENKA: What? I *am* worried, Ahmet. This is crazy.

MAJA: What's going on with Ahmet? Is that his name?

SUE: No, no. Is not just Ahmet. Is Ahmet Ahmetić!

MAJA: Senka's fiancé.

JIDU: Easy to remember.

EMIR: That's what I say!

SUE: Yes, very practical. I think she probably gonna divorce him. He doesn't care about her, trust me. Always excuses to avoid us.

EMIR: They not even married. Let it go!

SENKA: What do you mean they have the right to detain you? Okay, okay! Keep me posted. I love you too, *ljubavi*. Yes. Bye.

When SENKA *returns, everyone pretends to be busy.*

SENKA *grabs a bottle of pills from her purse and pops one in her mouth.*

SUE: What you are taking?

SENKA: Nothing. Prescriptions.

SUE: I hope everything okay with absent fiancé.

SENKA: I don't want to talk about it, *Majko bona* [dear mother].

SUE: He gonna be fine, *Senko*. He rich. He have lawyers.

SENKA: Ugh. You all heard?

MAJA: Why are they holding him back?

SUE: I told him to shave that beard.

JIDU: I have a beard.

SUE: You should shave it, too. Even worst for you, Jidu, trust me.

MAJA: That's absurd, Mama. A white man with a beard looks like a Greek god, but a Brown man with a beard is automatically suspect?

EMIR: Why you think I no have beard?

SUE: He not stupid. Muslim men must shave beard, that's how it is today.

MAJA: Bosniaks have no trouble crossing borders! They're white Muslims.

EMIR: Speak for yourself, *Majo*. You not a man who have to cross border during Siege of Sarajevo.

MAJA: I'm sorry, Tata. That was insensitive . . . you know what I meant.

SENKA: I'm worried about Ahmet. He's stuck in New York.

SUE: You no worry, *ljubavi*. They hold him back just for show. He gonna be back soon, you gonna see.

JIDU: Just a bump along the road to your happy marriage. When's the big day?

EMIR: When she finish her PH.D.

SUE: Not before. Another three years, *ako bog da* [God willing].

SENKA: How long can they legally detain someone in the States?

MAJA: I don't know.

SENKA: What if they search his phone? What if this turns into a case of Maher Arar?

JIDU: Whoa, whoa—it's never even going to get to that. Just a routine detain and question, that's all.

SUE: He Muslim. After 9/11, what you can expect?

SENKA: Mama . . .

EMIR: Your mother right. The world hate us, we must be careful and go inside the radar.

SENKA: Go *under* the radar.

EMIR: Even better!

SUE: This the worst time in history to be Muslim. *(to JIDU)* Religion was a private affair until they—*our neighbours*—start to kill us. Even though we grow up listening to Madonna and Michael Jackson, like other Europeans!

EMIR: I not even Muslim. I no believe in religion, not sure about God. But let me tell you the way it is in this world. *You* don't decide if you Muslim or not; other people decide for you. Ahmet, you think he decide he Muslim today? He wake up, check his email and get on plane. Maybe he think about Allah, maybe not. Maybe he pray, maybe not. But now that they have him, he become hard-core Muslim. They make him into one, just like they did to us during the war. We wake up, get dress, sometimes we pray to Allah when we want something or need forgiveness. But when war start, I no longer Emir Bolić, I just Muslim body—they decide for us how it is. That's it!

SUE: Why you say you no Muslim? They take everything from us—and now you *not* Muslim?

EMIR: Muslim people follow religion of Islam, that's what it mean. I never go to Mosque. I never pray. If there was God, what happen could never happen! End of story now! Where is Agata?

(shouting) Agata! *Dođi odma!* [Come immediately!]

AGATA: In a minute!

SUE: Okay, okay. Enough talking about Muslims, Emir! You gonna get sick again.

EMIR: Don't tell me if I Muslim or not Muslim. Nobody gonna tell me what I am and what I not! You hear me? There is no God if we can kill in his name and that's final! End of discussion!

EMIR slams the table, startling everyone.

MAJA: Okay, Tata, ease up a bit, please.

EMIR is suddenly disoriented.

EMIR: They take everything from me, everything.

SUE: *(to SENKA)* Go upstairs and get your sister. *(to MAJA)* You too, go, go now.

MAJA and SENKA exit.

JIDU: Maybe I should go with them?

EMIR: Leave the girls alone.

JIDU: Of course. *(beat)* Are you okay, Emir?

SUE: He gonna be fine. He just need a moment.

Awkward silence.

JIDU: The food is delicious, Sue. Truly.

SUE: Thank you, Jidu. *(beat)* So. What are you doing now?

JIDU: You mean for work?

SUE nods.

I'm a guitarist for a local band. We play rock and pop. It's gig work, a lot of weddings, some festivals. Spiritual Crisis—have you heard of us?

EMIR: Ha! What kind of band name is that?

JIDU: We came up with it years ago. It was either that or Thus Spoken from the Margins.

SUE: *Bože moj! Omladina poludila.* [My God! The younger generation has lost its mind.]

JIDU: My Bosnian's lousy.

EMIR: These are terrible band names, Jidu. Sorry, but it's true.

JIDU: To each their own, as they say.

SUE: No money in gig work.

JIDU: I recently bought a condo. Downtown.

EMIR: Huh!

SUE: How you can afford it?

JIDU: The condo fees are killing me!

EMIR: You end up paying rent *and* mortgage with those fees!

SUE: I'm happy to hear you make it, Jidu. I come listen to your band sometime.

EMIR grunts.

JIDU: I'd love that. Emir, I think you'd like us. We do covers.

EMIR: Not for me, thanks.

JIDU: You like the Beatles, right?

JIDU grabs his guitar.

EMIR: Who doesn't?

JIDU: Exactly. *(beat)* It's been a hard day's night?

EMIR doesn't bite.

(singing) And I've been working like a dog.

EMIR: *(speaking)* It's been a hard day's night.

JIDU: *(singing)* I should be sleeping like a log.

EMIR: This the best Beatle song. Really!

JIDU: I agree!

EMIR: What you know about working like dog?

JIDU: I respect hard work.

EMIR: Must be hard singing songs all day. Pfft!

SUE: Emir!

JIDU: I get it. You've had to work like a dog to make it in this country.

EMIR: *(grunts) Zove me psom u mojoj kući!* [He's calling me a dog under my own roof!]

JIDU: I'm sorry—what was that?

SUE: Jidu. Why you call my husband a dog?

JIDU: Pardon me? No! I am *not* calling you a dog, Emir!

EMIR: You say I like dog in this country.

JIDU: You *work* like a dog. Like in the Beatles song, you know?

EMIR: No Canadian gonna compare me to dog. I don't care if it's the best Beatle song in the world or what.

JIDU: Gosh, Emir. I was just . . . alluding to, you know.

EMIR: To what?

JIDU: You know, Maja . . . She . . . Um . . .

EMIR: My beautiful daughter Maja, yes. What about her?

JIDU: She told me you were an architect back home. How you're an educated man stuck in a working-class job.

EMIR: I see. Maja bring you here so you can insult me?

JIDU: Emir, look, I'm sorry.

EMIR: No! You right, Jidu! Construction in Berlin! Construction in Canada! Look at me. I'm like farm animal. Work, work, work till I can't feel my back!

JIDU: Maja's told me about your experience in Berlin . . .

SUE: That's why we come here—for better life.

SUE: Better life! This country did not recognize our university diplomas. Pfft.

JIDU: It's not right.

SUE: Oh, Jidu, you have no idea!

JIDU: You were an accountant back in Sarajevo, right?

SUE: I have master's degree and I a secretary serving coffee.

EMIR: My wife excellent at serving coffee.

SUE: *Zašto me ponižavaš pred njim?* [Why are you belittling me in front of him?]

EMIR: *Misliš da je tvoj posao više ponižavajući nego moj, ha?* [You think your job is more humiliating than mine, huh?]

JIDU: What are you saying?

EMIR: I don't understand why my daughter telling you about how poor and miserable we are?

JIDU: Emir, I mean—she never used those words. I—I'm sorry I gave that impression—Maja was just trying to explain how much the two of you have sacrificed so she could enjoy the life she has.

EMIR: I going to be sixty-four soon and I still making patios.

JIDU: Did you say sixty-four?

JIDU lifts his guitar once again.

SUE: No, Jidu.

EMIR: Not everything is happy Beatle song.

JIDU: Right. Sorry. What were you saying, Emir?

EMIR: I saying I sixty-four and who knows when I can afford to retire with Agata's university and my shitty pension plan.

JIDU: I'm sorry about that. You know, my grandparents went through similar experiences when they moved to the UK from India. They sacrificed everything so my parents could have an education and a better life.

EMIR: Immigrants break their backs here so their children can spend all day on MeTube.

JIDU: You mean YouTube?

EMIR: That's what I say.

SUE: It's hard for us to talk about these things, you understand?

JIDU: I can't imagine.

EMIR: Before war, life was good! Very good!

JIDU: I bet.

EMIR: I was hired by big firm in Sarajevo! We go on vacation by Adriatic Sea to celebrate! Drinking beer and eating corn at night. I still smell the salty waters, feel warm sand on my feet.

JIDU: Sounds romantic.

SUE: You would love Adriatic, Jidu. You must visit one day, during summer. Great local bands. The Balkans are alive with lights and music, especially by sea.

JIDU: I'd love that. "Kako si?" [How are you?]

SUE: *Dobro sam. Jel učiš bosanski?* [I'm good. Did you learn Bosnian?]

EMIR: No need to speak Bosnian to love the food! Remember that seafood restaurant? She get pregnant that summer.

SUE: No, Emir—I get pregnant the next year!

EMIR: Well, we make many beautiful babies—we good at it!

SUE and EMIR dance to a silent song only they can hear.

Suddenly, EMIR is stung by an invisible arrow. He experiences extreme chest pain.

Ahh!

SUE: What's wrong, my love?

EMIR: Nothing. I gonna sit on couch.

JIDU and SUE join him.

No point in remembering the good old days. And no more complaining about how hard life is here.

SUE: You right, Emir. We have everything here, Jidu. Nice home.

JIDU: Stunning house, really.

SUE: Three healthy daughters.

JIDU: Who could deny that?

SUE: I complain about being secretary but at least I have job!

EMIR: And our fridge always full!

JIDU: I've always eaten to my heart's content here.

SUE: We can't complain.

EMIR: No, we no gonna complain.

SUE: Thank God for Canada, that's what I always say: *hvala bogu* [thank God].

EMIR: Thank God we come here instead of staying in Germany.

SUE: It's in the past now. *(beat)* Jidu, can I get you anything? Wine? Beer? Rakija?

JIDU: I'm good, Sue, thank you. I'll help myself if I need anything.

EMIR: Please Jidu, you our guest. Sue gonna serve you.

MAJA, SENKA, and then AGATA enter. AGATA sports a short, androgynous haircut.

SUE: Oh, *majko mila* [dear mother]. What is this?

AGATA: Okay, Mama, don't freak out.

SENKA: I just found out five minutes ago, when she finally opened the door.

MAJA: You mean when we forced our way in?

SUE: Agata, *sine,* why you did this to me, why? Emir! Look at your daughter! Say something, *bolan*! Do something!

EMIR: Agata, *sine moj* [my child], you look like man.

SENKA: For a moment, Tata, I thought you'd *not* say something rude. *(to AGATA)* You look amazing.

JIDU: Oh my . . . Emir. The women in this family—are gorgeous. *(to AGATA)* You don't look like a man.

SUE: *O, majko mila!* [Oh, dear mother!]

AGATA: It's okay.

SUE: It's not okay, Agata. Did you know about this, Emir?

EMIR: Me? Leave me out of it. I not the reason your daughter decided to look like GI Joe.

SENKA: I think it suits her.

MAJA: She has the face for it!

EMIR: Enough. Let your mother handle this. Let's eat!

They all move to the dining room table.

SUE: Her beautiful long hair! Unbelievable. I never see a woman do this in my life. Never.

MAJA: Come on, Mama. Women have done more than cut their hair. They've shaved it all off: Natalie Portman, Charlize Theron, Demi Moore. Hello?

SUE pretends not to hear her.

SUE: Unbelievable . . .

MAJA: Happy birthday, by the way.

AGATA: Thank you for being here. I wasn't sure you'd come.

MAJA: I wouldn't miss it!

SENKA reacts with surprise and maybe a little bit of jealousy.

AGATA: And you too, Jidu. Haven't seen you since you guys broke up.

MAJA: Oh, no, we never dated.

JIDU: I mean, we've been very close since high school.

AGATA: Really?

MAJA: There are all kinds of relationships. Relationships are—you know—complicated.

SENKA: Well, this isn't awkward at all.

EMIR: We think he was a girl with all that hair, that's why he was allowed to come over, I remember that.

JIDU: I remember the day you figured out I was a guy. I took off my T-shirt and you were like, "What? You no have boobies? You boy! Holy shit!"

EMIR: I no speak like that. *(beat)* I say breast. I respect women and their parts, that's for sure.

The women roll their eyes and shake their heads.

JIDU: Sorry, Emir. I didn't mean to impersonate you. It just came out.

EMIR: Yeah well, everybody think you a girl.

SENKA: Who cares if you're a boy or a girl, right?

SUE: There is difference! One usually have long hair!

JIDU lets his hair down before lifting it back up in a ponytail.

JIDU: Some men have long hair, too.

SENKA: Boys, girls—it's all the same. *(to AGATA)* What do you think?

AGATA: I guess that's right. *(beat)* Now that we're all here, there's something I wanted to tell you—all of you.

SUE: After this?

AGATA: I've . . . um, I've decided to travel.

SUE: Travel?

EMIR: Where you going, *sine*?

AGATA: To Japan. With Barb. We're . . . umm . . .

SUE: Tsk, tsk, tsk! *Bože* . . . [God . . .]

EMIR: Great choice, honey. How are you going to get there, with what money?

AGATA: I saved up enough money and—

SUE: School start in September. Let your hair grow out while you gone that way no professor gonna see you like this.

SENKA: *Ma hajde, Majko.* [Come on, Mom.]

MAJA: I see students with all kinds of hair. Nobody cares.

AGATA: I'm leaving in June *(beat)* for a year.

SUE: First your hair now this—what next?

EMIR: Your mother is right. You can't leave for a year!

SUE: You already took year off to work. Now year off to travel? What's next, Agata, year off to paint?

JIDU: That'd be pretty cool.

EMIR: Mind your own business. This serious conversation.

SENKA: It *is* seriously annoying how you won't let her finish. Is that what you wanted to announce today, Gata?

Silence. Turbulence.

SUE: What announcement?

EMIR: She going to Japan!

MAJA: Oh, *that's* the announcement? God, I'm so airheaded lately. *(beat)* I'm happy for you, Gata. Go to Japan! Drink sake! Learn Japanese!

SENKA: Gata?

AGATA: I'm travelling with a friend . . . and . . .

SENKA: Yes?

SUE: So it already decided. You hear that, Emir? *Joj*, we give them everything. We travel halfway around the world for them, sacrifice our health and our bodies, and for what? So she can travel for year in Japan, *bože moj* [dear God]!

EMIR: You not going. That's final.

JIDU: But she's twenty years old.

EMIR: You a guest here so long as I allow it, remember that.

MAJA: Tata, come on. This is a big deal for Gata. I think we all need to slow down and appreciate her curiosity for other cultures, her appetite for travel.

SENKA: Right. *(beat)* Is there anything else you want to add, Gata?

SUE: *Ima još nešto da nam kaže?* [She has yet another thing to tell us?]

EMIR: *Kako je moguće?* [How is it even possible?]

MAJA: And when you're done, I'd like a moment to say something too.

AGATA: I just want you all to know that I already have the ticket. I'm leaving.

SUE: Allah!

MAJA: Alright. Well, then—

SUE: We gonna pay for your education. Happy birthday!

EMIR: We work like dogs and saving for years. For you. Your education. Key to good life.

AGATA: Thanks, Tata. I saved up my own money.

EMIR: Enough talk! We gonna have dinner. Today is a happy day, right? So let's be happy!

EMIR slams the table.

MAJA: *Tata bolan, šta ti je?* [Dad, what's wrong with you?] You scared me!

JIDU: You okay?

MAJA: Thank you, Jidu. I'm fine. You know what? I'm not fine.

SUE: This is storm day—what do you expect?

AGATA: Mama, listen. Tata, you too. I know you want me to go to university. But it's not my thing.

EMIR: You think it's "my *thing*" to be handyman, Gata? Please, child, don't talk about things you don't understand. Get an education, get good job.

SUE: Make good money, don't depend on man.

AGATA: I don't care about that stuff—money and marriage.

Beat.

MAJA: Well, then I might as well tell everyone now—

SENKA: Wait, Maja, don't steal her thunder.

AGATA: That's all I wanted to say.

MAJA: Okay, then—

SENKA: *Šta ti je, Majo* [What's up, Maja], can't you see Gata's trying to speak? A big shot professor and you don't have enough restraint to let her finish!

MAJA: *Šta je tebi, Senko?* [What about you, Senka?] A Ph.D. *student* who has *yet* to defend her thesis and you can't accept she's done talking?

AGATA: Don't bicker over me!

MAJA & SENKA: Don't tell me what to do!

MAJA: I came all this way to make an announcement!

SUE: Tell us what?

MAJA: I'm pregnant!

AGATA, SENKA, SUE: What?

JIDU is electrified from crown to toe.

EMIR: I can't believe it.

MAJA: Believe it, Tata. I'm four months in.

EMIR: The baby going to be half brown! Gonna look nothing like me.

SENKA: For the love of God, can you think before you speak?

AGATA: *(whispers)* It's racist, Tata.

EMIR: What? He not from India?

MAJA: He's Canadian!

JIDU: It's okay. If the baby were mine, it'd be brown. Nothing wrong with that, right Emir?

SUE: What you mean *if* the baby yours?

MAJA: He's not the father.

JIDU: I'm not the father?

EMIR: *Hvala bogu!* [Thank God!] A happy day! Yes! I'm going to be granddad. When we will meet the lucky man?

MAJA: That's the thing. There's no father.

JIDU, EMIR, SUE: What?

AGATA: Congratulations, Maja. I'm so happy for you.

SENKA: We're going to be aunts. What an amazing birthday present!

MAJA: Thank you.

AGATA: This is so exciting.

SUE: Oh, honey, I too young to be grandmother.

MAJA: Old enough, Mama!

EMIR: Everybody! I not done talking here!

JIDU: Congratulations, Maja! Congratulations, Sue and Emir!

JIDU drowns another shot of rakija.

MAJA: Don't you think you've had enough?

JIDU: I've had enough, that's for sure.

EMIR: Congratulations for what?

JIDU: You're going to be a grandfather, you lucky man!

EMIR: But how this could be, tell me, how? Who is father?

SUE: I bet he Canadian. They take no responsibility! It's all fun and games and travel!

JIDU: I'm not like that. But who cares about me, right?

MAJA: Mama, Tata, look: there's no dad.

JIDU: No dad . . .

SUE: Listen, *ljubavi*. We not children. We too old to believe in immaculate conception. What Muslim parent would believe that?

EMIR: Or atheist parent?

MAJA: I was artificially inseminated.

EMIR: What? This artificial baby?

MAJA: No. Oh my God!

EMIR: I don't understand, Maja! Real baby must have father!

MAJA: Mine will only have a mom.

EMIR: But how it's possible?

MAJA: Sperm bank!

EMIR: I was wrong. God is real, and this is His hand *(lifts arm)* coming down to smite me. *(slams table)* Sperm bank! What is this bullshit? You need man and woman to make baby. That's how it is in nature.

MAJA: Unbelievable!

EMIR: Tell me if you see horses or dogs going to sperm bank to make babies? Hah? You see that anywhere?

SENKA: Wow, Tata. You just compared Maja to a horse *and* a dog.

AGATA: I'm sure he didn't mean it like that.

EMIR: I did!

AGATA: Tata, c'mon.

EMIR: I meant every word I say!

AGATA: Maja's finally home.

EMIR: What I say again?

SUE: Forget him—listen to your mother, Maja. You are beautiful woman. You a professor, for God sake! You make a lot of money. I know for sure you can find good man!

MAJA: I don't know what I was thinking coming back here. I should have called or written.

MAJA feels stuck in a barbed wire snare. She shifts places and JIDU follows.

JIDU: Stay at my place.

MAJA: *Ich hasse das.* [German: I hate this.]

SENKA: *Willkommen zuhause, große Schwester.* [German: Welcome home, big sis.]

JIDU: Ignore me, then.

MAJA: Jidu, do you seriously need my attention right now?

JIDU: No! You're home. I'm happy. It's tense in here. You just—I mean—I don't know what to say! *(beat)* You're pregnant!

MAJA: So?

JIDU: So you said you were waiting to be ready.

MAJA: And I did—I waited till I was ready. *(trying to be discrete)* I told you it was just fucking.

SUE: *(to EMIR)* Oh, Allah.

JIDU: Fine! Great! I hope you're happy.

MAJA: I am.

JIDU: Good. Then it's all good.

AGATA: Do you guys need privacy?

MAJA: No. *(to JIDU)* You can go home if you want.

SUE: You stay, Jidu. We happy to see you, right Emir?

EMIR: What?

AGATA: I'm glad you're here.

SENKA: You keep us grounded.

MAJA: *(in disbelief)* Great—wonderful!

JIDU: Well, I guess there's still cake coming, right?

SUE: I make *šampita* and baklava.

JIDU: I remember those.

EMIR: I order some *Bienenstich* from Polish store.

JIDU: What's that?

EMIR: Bee sting cake, German specialty.

MAJA: Jidu, you're staring at me.

JIDU: Maybe because I'm in love with you.

AGATA: Aww . . .

MAJA: Let it go, Jidu. We can talk later.

JIDU: Okay . . . but you owe me.

MAJA: Owe you what?

JIDU: An explanation, Maja.

MAJA remembers the fragrance of the hours spent with JIDU.

MAJA: Okay. Later, I promise.

SUE: I don't understand why you not tell me sooner you planning to do this, *Majo sine.*

MAJA: I'm not the only one keeping secrets!

AGATA: Well, some secrets are hard to talk about.

SUE: Ok, *sine.* Let's play nice. *(to MAJA)* How come you not use sperm of a man you know, *ljubavi*?

EMIR: Why you no—*you know*—with a man, like normal person?

MAJA: The thing about you two is that you treat us all like children.

SUE: What she is saying?

SENKA: Stop pretending you don't understand. You infantilize us.

EMIR: What this word mean?

AGATA: We talked about it a few weeks ago over dinner when you told me to wash my hands and not forget to dry them.

EMIR: I have no idea what dinner you talking about.

SUE: The dinner Ahmet Ahmetić not come to, remember?

SENKA: Why do you insist upon saying his name in full?

SUE: That not his name? You think I stutter or what?

SENKA is speechless. Kilometres of raw feelings spill from her mouth.

Senka *sine*, it's not me who highlight his name. Listen to this! I write his name on computer when I make seating arrangements. First Ahmet, then, second Ahmet, and before I even finish, spell check want me to delete his name. *(beat)* It say to me "Delete repeated word." Even Microsoft Word cannot process his name!

AGATA: *(laughs)* I'm sorry, that's not funny.

SENKA: I'm amazed you decided to create place cards, Mama, considering you've never done that before in your entire life.

SUE: Is just silly name tags.

SENKA: And then in Ahi's absence, you insisted on keeping it at the table so you could spend forty-five minutes *(to MAJA)*—I kid you not, forty-five whole minutes—commenting on my fiancé's name.

AGATA: Yep, I remember that.

EMIR: I was not at this meeting.

SENKA: It wasn't a meeting, Tata! It was a dinner.

AGATA: Ivan was there.

EMIR: Ivan was there?

SUE: What is this, Emir? Stop joking, *bolan*. You get so drunk you almost vomit, remember? Maybe you have too many tonight already.

EMIR: Enough talking. Bring out the cake.

SUE: What about dinner?

MAJA: I'm not hungry.

SENKA: Me neither, I've lost all appetite.

EMIR: Okay, then, it's cake time.

SUE: What about all my cooking?

EMIR: Forget it.

AGATA: I'll clear the table and bring out the desert.

SENKA: I'll join you.

SUE: Unbelievable.

AGATA and SENKA exit.

JIDU: Let me help.

EMIR: You stay here. *(to SUE)* You see? At least we raised those two right.

MAJA: What's that supposed to mean?

JIDU: Maybe we all need to take a chill pill, slow down a bit.

EMIR: Take pills? She bring pusher into my house?

JIDU: It's an expression. It means to take it easy, you know?

SUE: Look, kid, we Balkan. This is how we relax.

JIDU: Right, it's a Bosnian thing. The Bolić family is relaxing.

MAJA: It's not a cultural difference, Mama, it's an excuse.

EMIR: You be careful. You're already in trouble, young woman! How dare you go to sperm bank without my permission?

MAJA: I'm thirty-four years old! I don't need your permission to do anything.

SUE: Honey, *ljubavi, Majo moja* [my love, my Maja], you my first daughter. I care for you like rare jewel. I was in labour for thirty-six hours and—

MAJA: Mama. Spare me.

EMIR: Yes, please. We hear it before, many times.

SUE: It's your fault she done this! After being raised by man like you, of course she go to sperm bank.

EMIR: What? Don't blame me! You the mother. You raise them. You forget to teach them right from wrong.

MAJA: You don't have to agree with my decision, but I will not take this kind of belittling. Agata and Senka may be used to it, but I'm not.

SUE: *(innocently)* Couldn't you find man, *ljubavi*?

MAJA: Goddamnit, Mama, I wasn't looking for one.

JIDU: Yeah! She wasn't looking for one!

EMIR: What you are going to tell the child?

MAJA: The truth. They're a donor baby.

EMIR: Pffft! A donor baby! He needs man, real man, father who is there to provide.

SUE: *Ma da bolan* [Yes], provide what?

EMIR: We are men! We take care of our families, our children, our wives.

SUE: How many diapers you change in your life, hah? How many doctor appointments you take them to, tell me, please?

A pained expression runs across SUE's face, a heartbreaking memory.

EMIR: You see, Jidu, it always like that, my whole life. Four against one.

JIDU: Don't look at me, man.

EMIR: Fine! Fine! You all against me now.

SUE: I do everything for my children. You no have right complain about my parenting, Emir! How dare you? Sometimes things happen a mother cannot control. That's my pain.

MAJA experiences a sudden PTSD flashback.

MAJA: Oh, God. I don't feel good. *(holds belly)*

EMIR: *(confused)* What I was saying? *(puts hand on heart)* Oh, it stings.

MAJA: It's freezing.

SUE: Turn up the heat.

EMIR turns up the heat. His gestures are lost, vacant, empty.

AGATA and SENKA enter with plates and desserts.

AGATA: What's going on? You all look so serious.

SUE: It's fine, honey. Don't worry. Your father need a break from speaking. So do I.

AGATA: Senka can't find the candles for the cake, Mama, where are they?

SUE: I don't know, *ljubavi*, in drawer by fridge?

SENKA: They're not there.

JIDU: You alright, Sue? You look like you just saw a ghost.

SUE: I fine! But Maja look pale. I go get you sweater. Take break from your father!

MAJA: *Hvala ti, Majko.* [Thank you, Mom.]

Momentary silence. Everyone's faces grow sad and pensive.

They are islands standing together-apart until SUE returns.

SUE: Here, *Majo*, remember this sweater I pass down to you when you live with us?

MAJA: Mama! I hated that thing when I was seventeen.

SUE: I thought maybe you like it now. I make myself when I was in university, just after I met your father.

MAJA: Oh . . . Okay, I'll try it on.

MAJA puts it on and looks very silly. SENKA and AGATA chuckle.

AGATA: It's nice an' colourful. It's even got some pink—your favourite colour.

SENKA: It screams, "Hello, I'm a hard-core feminist."

MAJA: Oh—I missed you two, I really did.

SENKA: We missed you too . . .

SUE: Eight years a long time, *Majo moja,* without your family. *(about the sweater)* Not so bad, hah?

JIDU: It could be worse.

MAJA takes off the sweater.

MAJA: It's—it's the wool. It's itchy. Sorry, Mama.

EMIR: Enough, Suzo. Leave her alone. She a grown woman.

MAJA: Listen, Mama. I'm touched, I really am. Why don't I take it with me and—and ahh—

JIDU: And she'll give it to her future child, right?

MAJA: Right! Yes, that's right.

SUE: This is excellent idea!

MAJA: Can't believe you've kept this old sweater for so long.

SENKA: It's got this vintage eighties vibe.

SUE: That's because I make it in eighties. It was long time ago. I still love it.

MAJA: Well . . . thank you.

SUE: I still shocked at the big news.

EMIR: What big news?

AGATA: *The news*, Tata. Maja's big announcement.

EMIR: What, you no share things with your tata?

SENKA: Are you serious?

MAJA: You don't remember the good news I announced this evening?

EMIR: I remember Agata's bad news.

AGATA: Travelling's not bad news, Tata!

EMIR: Ha! Where you get that? On Facepage?

SENKA: Tata, answer the question. What did Maja announce tonight?

EMIR: She not announce anything tonight except that she cold. *Ma pustite me na miru, bolan.* [Leave me alone.]

SUE: You see what I have to deal with? You see?

SENKA: Tata?

EMIR: Your mother is driving me crazy, *sine*.

SUE: Must be nice to have selective memory!

EMIR: If only I could select you out, *ljubavi*!

SENKA: Tata, this evening Maja told us she was pregnant.

EMIR proudly shakes JIDU's hand.

EMIR: Congratulations! I'm so happy.

JIDU: No, man, I'm not the father.

EMIR: *(to MAJA) Dušo moja* [my soul], I'm so happy.

MAJA: That'd been nice twenty minutes ago.

EMIR: What other reaction can there be? My heart is full. I going to be grandfather! *Suzo moja* [My Sue], you hear that? Our child is pregnant.

SUE: There's no father.

EMIR: What?

MAJA: Intrauterine insemination.

EMIR: Intra-what? Is this GMO baby?

AGATA: No, Tata. It's when you buy sperm online and the doctors at the fertility clinic . . . you know.

EMIR: What? No! You go back to that fertility clinic and you ask for refund right away, *sine*.

AGATA: It's not a pair of jeans, Tata.

EMIR: Who is father?

SENKA: Anonymous sperm donor.

EMIR: Where he is from?

MAJA: The United States of America.

SUE: Oh, my God! An American baby! What have we done, Allah, what have we done?

MAJA: Who cares where the donor is from? The baby will be Canadian, like me.

SENKA: Well—Bosnian Canadian.

MAJA: Whatever! Canadian! Bosnian! Muslim! Atheist! Do we need these categories? And whose side are you on anyway, Senka?

SUE: She on the side of common sense, *Majo*! Why you make baby with American donor, hah? To punish us?

EMIR: And why you not call your tata to ask permission?

MAJA: We already went through this. I feel like a broken record.

EMIR: Fine! I gonna go out for smoke.

SENKA: Wait. How long have you been forgetting things?

EMIR: I no forget, Senka. Leave me alone and don't block your father's way.

EMIR exits.

JIDU: He forgot his coat! I'll be right back, excuse me.

JIDU exits.

SENKA: What a nice guy.

AGATA: Thoughtful and kind. I really like him.

MAJA: Stop it, you two. I don't have space for this.

SENKA: *(to SUE)* It could be early onset Alzheimer's or dementia. Is he taking any medication that can cause memory loss?

SUE: Who, your father? Don't be fooled, *ljubavi*. He manipulating, nothing more.

AGATA: Could it be trauma? I read it can do that.

MAJA: Oh?

SUE: What trauma? If anyone should be forgetting, it's me. *(hands up in prayer)* Allah, please bless me with selective memory loss! What blissful state of surrender that would to be!

SENKA: If it's trauma-related, then something must have triggered it. Mama? When did the memory lapses begin?

SUE: Maybe four months ago?

SENKA: What happened?

SUE: What happen? Let me see: I prepare his lunch and his dinner. He come home and watch TV until 9 p.m. and then he go to bed. He wake up before me, leave for work the next day. That's our life! No life at all!

SENKA: Yeah, okay, I didn't mean *that*. Did something weird happen, something outside of the norm?

SUE: *Čekaj bona* [Wait], I know. I remember now. It wasn't four months ago! It was six months ago that woman start to work with him! Now we have proof he's cheating on me!

MAJA: Come on. You've been saying that your whole life.

SUE: This time it's true.

SENKA: If nothing happened this year, did anything upsetting happen in October in the past?

SUE: *Ne. Nemoguće.* [No. Impossible.]

SENKA: What? What's impossible?

MAJA: My stomach is acting up.

SENKA: You okay?

MAJA: I have to go to the bathroom. Excuse me.

MAJA exits.

SENKA: Can you think of anything, hah?

SUE: Nothing! Your dad and I never talk about past. That's how it is, he say. We no talk about it.

AGATA: Yep, that's him. *(imitates his voice)* "That's it! No more story!"

SENKA: But don't you think that's strange?

AGATA: I never thought about it. Maja's the same. So are you, Mama.

SUE: Sometimes it's better that way, trust me.

SENKA: Alright, okay. So you're sure nothing happened at all, nothing he's told you?

SUE: You may gonna be psychologist one day, *ljubavi Senko*, but you no good at listening. Your father is a-messing behind my back and I nobody's fool.

SENKA: Aah! Mama! Cheating's not head trauma!

SUE: Excuse me? Of course, it very traumatic if he cheat on me! I the love of his life! And I gonna file for divorce; he know it. I gonna do it, you just watch!

AGATA: Mama, Senka's just trying to help. You know Tata best. He can't hide anything from you.

SUE: Nothing happen last October.

SENKA: Then when?

SUE: Don't talk about things you don't know.

SENKA: You're impossible! I'm tired—I give up.

Angrily, almost unconsciously, SENKA *puts on the sweater.*

SUE: The past is dead. It's over.

AGATA: *(to* SENKA*)* You shouldn't be so hard on her, you know. And that sweater looks horrible on you.

SENKA: Hard on her? Who's hard on her? I'm trying to help. I'm cold! And I'm pissed!

AGATA: I get it, okay? You're stressed. I'm stressed.

SUE: You brute, *Senko*, just like your father!

SENKA: If you won't tell us what happened then we'll just pretend he's cheating on you and call it a night.

AGATA: Whoa, Senka. Do you have to be so mean?

SENKA: Me? Mean? What should I do, Gata? Be like you and beat around the bush instead of speaking frankly?

AGATA: That's not fair. You know how hard it is for me to open up.

SENKA: I'm suffocating in here.

SENKA goes on her cell phone. EMIR and JIDU enter.

EMIR: What is it, Suzo? What is it, *Senko*? Agata?

Tense silence.

JIDU: Is it just me or is it cake time?

MAJA enters.

EMIR: We eat when I say it's time. *(to SENKA)* You look funny with that sweater on. You cold? I gonna turn up the heat some more.

Nobody responds.

(to SUE) What's wrong, woman? Why you standing there like statue?

SUE: Why you don't put away Maja's luggage to her room while we finish setting table?

EMIR: *(to JIDU)* You can pick those up, I gonna show you to the room.

JIDU: I'm only his errand boy because it's your luggage, Maja.

MAJA: *(sighs)* Thanks.

EMIR and JIDU exit.

SUE: I gonna go to kitchen. Bring more drinks and food.

SUE exits.

SENKA takes off the sweater, gives it to AGATA, who puts it on for fun.

The three sisters sit together. SENKA hits the lamp with her elbow.

SENKA: Ow!

MAJA: What a piece of shit, this lamp.

AGATA: Senka.

SENKA: Yes?

AGATA: You were right.

SENKA: About what?

AGATA: The reason I emailed you—both of you—it wasn't related to Japan.

SENKA: I knew it!

MAJA: Oh, gosh! Gata. I stole your thunder, didn't I?

SENKA: I won't say I told you so.

MAJA: I'm sorry.

AGATA: I'm glad you did. It took the light off me for a second.

Pause.

Senka?

SENKA: Yep?

AGATA: I'm freaking out. Give me one of your anxiety pills, please.

SENKA: Just breathe, Agata, you'll be fine. That sweater *actually* looks good on you.

AGATA: I'm super stressed out. C'mon, please, pretty please?

SENKA takes out a bottle of pills from her purse.

SENKA: Okay, but only because this is an exceptional time. Do not ever ask me again, you hear me?

AGATA: Yes, I promise.

AGATA pops a pill.

I don't feel anything.

SENKA: Give it twenty.

MAJA: What is it?

SENKA: What do you think? Klonopin.

MAJA: And you just carry that around in your purse? Do you have anxiety or something?

SENKA: Yes—Maja—your powers of deduction are amazing. I suffer from anxiety.

Stiff silence.

MAJA: *(to AGATA)* Why is she so angry?

AGATA: I don't know. You know how she is. She's trying to help but is going about it the wrong way.

SENKA: I'm right here, Gata! The two of you don't need to speak of me in the third person.

MAJA: Why are you pissed at me?

SENKA: You leave for eight years—eight whole years—and you're asking me why I'm pissed?

MAJA: *Senko*, listen, I'm sorry I've been chronically absent. You're my little sister and I know—

SENKA: You were supposed to come to my graduation, then my engagement party—

MAJA: I know! I haven't been there for you. I'm sorry. I'm really, very sorry.

SENKA: It's fine, I already told you, it's fine. You had other obligations that were more important than your family.

MAJA: You know it's not like that. *Volim te, bona, Senko.* [I love you, Senka.]

SENKA: It's fine. I don't know what else you want me to say. And don't tell me you love me! You love Agata. She emails you once and—poof—you're here.

MAJA: You're angry, I get it. But you don't have to be so harsh.

SENKA: You're right. I didn't mean that. You're not here for Agata. You're here for yourself—to tell the parents you're pregnant and then disappear for another eight years.

MAJA: Okay . . . fine! I'm selfish! You don't mean anything to me. Neither does Agata!

AGATA: Oh, man . . . you guys, this sucks. I just wish we could clear the air.

MAJA: How very Canadian of you, Gata.

AGATA: I never say the right thing.

SENKA: *(grunts)* It's not you, Gata. Ahmet's not responding to any of my texts. I don't even know why I got so mad at Mom.

MAJA: Can a pregnant woman take these pills safely?

SUE: *(from kitchen) Senko, hajde da mi pomogneš, molim te!* [Senka, come help me, please!]

SENKA: *(looking through purse)* I don't have anything for you, Maja. Forget the Klonopin. You're pregnant, it's not worth the risk. Wait—let me see . . .

SUE: *(from kitchen) Senkooo*!

SENKA: Coming, Mama! *(on her way to the kitchen)* Take some vitamin C pills, if you want. The ones in the big blue bottle.

SUE: Seeenko! *Hajde, bona!* [Come on!]

SENKA: Coming, Mama! You know—I'm glad you're home. But, for the record, you're kinda like the parents. There's always a feeling like you're far away even when you're around. Even now.

MAJA: Thanks *(beat)* I guess . . .

SENKA exits.

I broke her heart when I left, didn't I?

AGATA: Hard core. And she holds grudges, you know how she is.

MAJA: So, little sis—what is this big news that compelled you to write to me begging for my presence?

MAJA pops a pill.

It's not like you to write more than a paragraph and remain so mysterious.

AGATA: I know. I was a bit dramatic. I honestly didn't think you'd come.

MAJA: Yet here I am, in the flesh.

EMIR and JIDU enter. EMIR claps suddenly, startling his daughters.

EMIR: Okay, my darlings. Please sit down around table. We gonna celebrate Agata's birthday properly. No more distractions.

MAJA: *(to AGATA)* Saved by the bell.

JIDU: Twenty, that's a great year.

EMIR: *(to AGATA)* Where's your mother?

AGATA: In the kitchen.

EMIR: Go help her.

AGATA: Senka's already helping her. There's something I have to tell you when she gets here.

SENKA enters the room with a bottle of champagne.

EMIR: Fine, that's good, *ljubavi*. I hope you gonna tell us you going to university in September.

AGATA: God, Tata, you make me so angry sometimes.

EMIR: You too, *ljubavi*.

SUE enters.

SUE: Okay everybody. I don't know where the candles go. Emir, you know where they are?

EMIR: Why you ask me? I not the woman here.

SENKA: Tata!

AGATA: Please filter!

MAJA: Oh my God, Tata—you are *incorrigibly* sexist!

EMIR: You should be a-shame to talk to your father like that. You no even know how to make baby with man and you tell me how to talk to my wife, unbelievable.

MAJA: I'm not fucking ashamed of my choices! *You* should be embarrassed! Look at yourself, look at your life! *(to SUE)* And you—look at the way Tata treats you!

SUE: Your father crazy, *Majo moja.* You know that. He careless with everything, his wife and his children!

MAJA: Oohh!

MAJA experiences a sudden and overwhelming PTSD flashback.

Suggestion: sounds of bombing, but no sniper shots.

JIDU: Breathe, Maja, breathe. In and out, yes, like that.

SENKA grabs her wrist.

EMIR: What is all this?

SENKA: Her heart rate is off the charts!

AGATA: Call an ambulance!

SUE: Emir, your daughter need you now.

MAJA is lost, as if held captive by the flashback.

MAJA: We're going to lose him.

JIDU: Look at me, Maja. There. There. Listen to me, you're not going to lose anyone tonight. Trust me.

EMIR: *(suddenly regaining his vigour)* Move, everyone, move. I gonna drive her.

SUE: No! You drunk.

EMIR: You too drunk to know whether I drunk or not.

MAJA: Why did I come here?

SENKA: *(looking through her bag)* What pill did you take, Maja? The vitamin C or—or the other one?

SUE: What pill?

MAJA: It's not the pill. It's—it's the atmosphere in here.

SUE: It's your father.

MAJA: It's both of you.

JIDU: Can you walk?

MAJA: Oohhh . . .

JIDU: *(to SUE)* Get her coat, her hat, her boots. Now.

EMIR: This is my daughter. I gonna take care of it.

JIDU: Emir, let me drive. I'm more sober.

EMIR: I the man of the family here.

JIDU has a silent standoff with EMIR.

Okay, you gonna drive. I allow it!

JIDU: Let's go.

SENKA: Hurry!

AGATA: Senka, give them the bottle of pills we took. Just in case.

MAJA: Agata, I'm sorry, your party—

AGATA: No—please—take care of the baby!

SENKA: Here. I don't know which bottle she tried. This blue one or *(beat)* this blue one. Oh, God! They're both blue. She . . . I think she might have taken one of these a few minutes ago. I was sure the vitamin C was in a different coloured bottle . . . oh God, I'm so sorry.

SUE: Shame on you! Giving your pregnant sister medication!

EMIR: Shame! Shame! You ask why we in-fen-ti-la . . . in-fen-ta li-taz you! Because you all act like children. Playing with pills like they dolls.

MAJA, JIDU, SUE, and EMIR exit.

ACT 2

Several hours later.

SENKA: *(stroking sweater)* Even when we were little, I couldn't stop fighting with her. She was always their favourite.

AGATA: We all fought all the time. We still do!

SENKA: I've been mad at her since she left us—*she left us!* With *them!*

AGATA: You took that personally?

SENKA: I don't know. Maybe.

AGATA: Aw, Senka. It wasn't your fault. You know how Maja is.

SENKA: At least we don't have it as bad as Jidu. I don't understand why he just doesn't move on.

AGATA: Beats me.

EMIR suddenly barges in, followed by SUE.

A few seconds later MAJA enters followed by JIDU.

EMIR: I tell you, woman, let her be! You hear me?

SUE: Let *her* be? And what else, Emir? Let *you* be, right?

In the background, JIDU and MAJA talk in sign language with SENKA and AGATA to let them know MAJA and the baby are all right.

EMIR: You heard the doctor! You need to calm down, woman!

SUE: The doctor, the doctor! Why you don't stand up for your wife like real man?

EMIR: What wife? I'm married to witch!

SUE: Cursed be the day I marry you, Emir!

EMIR: You no curse me, Suzo. I had enough! Uggh, I going out for smoke!

SUE: We just walk in!

EMIR: I can't breathe in here.

SUE: How convenient. You have your cigarette! You come and go as you want! What about me, hah? I stuck in here like bird in a jail.

EMIR: A bird? What bird, *bona*? You hear gentle singing anywhere? More like wild tiger!

SUE: You bet I more like wild tiger. You can no domesticate me.

EMIR: Ha! You hear that? Everyone hear her, right? Now we know who is real beast in this house.

SUE: Oh, please, Emir. I too exhausted to fight with you.

EMIR: I going out.

EMIR exits.

MAJA: Thank God. I don't have any more energy for Mama's and Tata's fighting.

SUE: *Sine,* it's not me, I swear to Allah! *(hands open in prayer) O, majko moja mila, šta sam ja uradila dragom bogu da mi da takvog muža?* [Dear mother, what have I done to God to give me a husband like him?]

AGATA: It's okay, Mama.

SUE: It's no gonna be okay.

MAJA: I'm going to bed. *Please* don't knock on my door before I'm up in the morning.

SENKA: Do you need anything?

MAJA: Peace, Senka, I need peace and quiet.

MAJA exits.

SENKA: *(very dry tone)* What happened?

SUE: What happen? Ask your father what happen.

SENKA: *(to JIDU)* So?

JIDU: They got into a fight on the way there, at the hospital, *(beat)* and on the way home.

SENKA: Of course they did.

AGATA: Aw, Mama. Is Maja okay?

SUE: They say she had panic attack! Because of us! Can you believe it?

SENKA: Oh goodness, because of the pill?

JIDU: No, no. She means Emir and her.

SUE: Crazy doctors! Crazy! She become sick before you father and me fight on the way to hospital.

AGATA: Poor Maja.

SUE: Yes! Poor Maja! Poor me! Poor all of us. Your father is impossible!

SENKA: It takes two to tango.

SUE: What you are saying?

SENKA: I'm saying there's a dynamic between the two of you, a certain chemistry.

SUE: There's no chemistry! It's just anger and frustration!

SENKA: That's exactly what I'm saying. *Smiri se, molim te.* [Calm down, please.]

SUE: Don't tell me to calm down, child.

SENKA: You heard Maja. She needs peace and quiet.

SUE: Nobody hear me, nobody cares!

AGATA: *Majko,* Mama, hey, hey, what's going on? Why are you so upset?

SUE: Your sister want to name her unborn child Abaz.

AGATA & SENKA: Abaz?

AGATA: Is that a boy name?

SUE: Yes! Yes, it is! Abaz! She can choose any boy name and she choose Abaz!

SENKA: So, it's a boy! Abaz—great!

SUE: This is not great, *Senko moja.* Not at all.

SENKA: I don't get it. Why are you so agitated?

JIDU: That's nothing, man. Shoulda heard 'em in emerg. It's a good thing we were already at the hospital. With the way they were carrying on, one of them was going to need a gurney.

SUE: You were gentleman. Take such good care of our daughter. Too bad you not the father.

JIDU: Too bad, so sad, right?

SUE: Maybe she not sexual?

JIDU: She's definitely sexual.

SUE: How you know that?

JIDU looks away.

SENKA: It really *is* too bad you're not the father, Jidu.

AGATA: Why don't I make some tea, huh? It'll calm the nerves.

SUE: I'll have coffee. Turkish. Thank you, *sine.*

AGATA: Okay, one Turkish coffee comin' right up.

SENKA: Let me do it. I need some space.

SENKA exits.

JIDU: *(holds up guitar)* Now—any requests?

AGATA: Hmm . . . how about "Closer"?

JIDU: I love Tegan and Sara!

JIDU strums.

AGATA: Barb loves Tegan and Sara . . .

SUE: Barb loves Tegan and Sara! *Sine*, listen to me: friends like that are distractions. Go to university, make something of your life!

AGATA: Barb may be many things, but she's *not* a distraction.

SUE: Then what she is, *ljubavi*? She the one who influence you to take another year off, no? Waste of time and money, trust me!

AGATA: Mama, listen. Barbara is my partner, my girlfriend.

SUE: What are you saying?

AGATA: Mama. I love her. I'm *in love* with her. We're going to live together in Tokyo.

SENKA enters.

SENKA: Here's your coffee. *(beat)* What is it?

JIDU: Excuse me. I'm just going to step out a bit. Let you speak privately. I'm worried about Emir.

SUE: Don't tell him, please. Today's not good day.

SENKA: Tell him what?

JIDU: I won't. But someone's got to prepare him. The mood he's in right now . . . oh, man.

JIDU exits.

SENKA: *(to AGATA)* You all right?

AGATA: Say something, Mama.

SUE: How long this been going on?

AGATA: Two years.

SUE: You have a secret that I not know about for two years?

AGATA: It's not like that, *Majko*.

SUE: You see, *Senko*? Everyone keeping secrets from me.

AGATA: Oh, Mama, I'm sorry. I couldn't tell you—I just couldn't tell anyone.

SUE: *I am your mother.*

Brief pause.

AGATA: Senka, Barb's my girlfriend. My girlfriend, girlfriend.

SENKA: I know.

SUE: How you know?

SENKA: It's been obvious since she was fourteen.

SUE: *Kako to?* [How's that?]

SENKA: Remember Sandy?

SUE: Her best friend?

AGATA: Ex-best friend . . .

SENKA: It was obvious you and Sandy were more than just best friends.

SUE: Unbelievable! Allah! What is going on right in my nose?

AGATA: *Under* your nose.

SUE: What? *Sine!* Where *you* been putting that nose of yours, huh? Allah!

SENKA and AGATA hug.

SENKA: Love you, li'l sis.

AGATA: Love you too, *Senko.*

SUE: Your father gonna freak out.

AGATA: I know, that's why I couldn't say it earlier.

SUE: I guess it's in your genes to hide and sneak around—just like him.

SENKA: Mama! For once, this isn't about you or Tata!

EMIR and JIDU enter.

EMIR: What now?

JIDU: Emir, why don't you take a seat?

EMIR: I'm okay. You are our guest, Jidu—please accept my apology for being rude with you earlier. Can I get you anything, a beer?

JIDU: No, thanks. Maybe a tea?

EMIR: What kind?

JIDU: Mint would be awesome.

EMIR: Mint is the best. *(looks at SUE)* I will make it for you myself!

SENKA: That's lovely, Tata.

EMIR: What?

SENKA: Your hospitality.

EMIR: This man here take my daughter to hospital in less than ten minutes in middle of the worst storm of the year. He talk to doctor and nurses when they were gonna call security on your mother. He is my guest here tonight and can stay as long as he likes. That's it!

JIDU: Thanks, Emir. I'm touched.

EMIR: Mint! Mint! Good choice.

EMIR exits.

JIDU: He's not in a good mood, I warn you.

SENKA: He looks better than when you walked into the house.

SUE: I know him. He's brew on the inside.

JIDU: If I may, Sue . . . May I?

SUE nods.

Maybe you should talk to him before Agata tells him.

AGATA: Excellent idea!

SUE: *Bože dragi* [Dear God], what I gonna to say? This horrible news. Worse than the hair, worse than the sperm baby!

AGATA: I promised Barb I'd do it, but this is the worst day to come out! I should have waited longer. I just—Maja's here and I thought . . . If I don't do it now, I'll never find the courage.

SENKA: You did the right thing, Gata. And anyway: is there *ever* a good day . . . with them?

SUE: I cannot accept this! We gonna find you a good Bosnian man, Agata, trust me. I have lots of friends with single sons. You can pick effeminate one. How about Suleiman, Teta Aida's son, huh? He's very tall, kind of strange actually, but, hey—really smart, good potential.

AGATA: Mama, come on.

SUE: *(to JIDU)* Why not you marry Agata? She look just like Maja, except younger, hah? Less hair, less hassle.

JIDU: Okay, Sue, now you're talking nonsense.

SENKA: What's wrong with you, Mama?

SUE: What's wrong with you, Senka? You gonna be psychologist. You help your sister, okay?

SENKA: You're the one that needs help, not Gata. Face it, Mama: your daughter is a beautiful lesbian.

SUE: *(horrified)* You corrupt your little sister! You devil!

SENKA: You're the devil!

AGATA: Please, Mama, Senka, stop. For me.

SENKA: She's homophobic!

SUE: You call me Islam-phobic last week—now you call me homophobic! What's next, *Senko*, huh?

SENKA: Don't deflect, Mama. *(beat)* I said you have *internalized* Islamophobia—it's not the same.

SUE: You mother-phobic, *Senko moja*! The only cure is for you to listen to me! Listen to your mother for once!

SENKA: You can't help it, can you? I can't believe we turned out so well considering how backward you are.

AGATA: Senka! Come on, man.

SENKA: That's it, I'm done.

SUE: You breaking my heart, all of you!

SENKA: You're not the victim here.

SUE: First Maja have baby with herself and now this. How I not the victim here?

SENKA: Don't bully your daughters! Respect our choices. There's nothing wrong with Ahmet! *(beat)* I mean Barb, goddamnit, there's nothing wrong with Agata loving Barb!

AGATA: I can't do this anymore.

SUE: I not the bad guy here! I want my daughters to get married and have beautiful, normal families.

SENKA: Arg! I don't know why I bother.

AGATA: Listen, Mama, Barb and I have talked about having children.

SUE: What? Another daughter who have baby without man? This too much for my heart, my soul.

SENKA: Mama! Think before you speak!

JIDU: *(to SENKA)* All right, come on, folks . . .

SUE: Any normal mother would react like me.

SENKA: There's nothing normal about your behaviour!

AGATA: Enough! I was prepared for Mama's rejection, but not for this. I can't stand this kind of fighting. Enough! I've had enough!

SENKA: Damn it, Gata! Everything's not about you, okay?

AGATA: You're just like them, Senka!

SENKA: You're right! I know I'm just like them. Why do you think I wanted to become a shrink in the first place?

Brief pause.

JIDU: You're okay, Senka. You're doing your best, standing up for what's right.

SUE: Stay out of it, Jidu!

AGATA: Let's be kind to each other, please.

EMIR enters and gives JIDU his tea.

EMIR: Why you screaming? I leave for five minutes and already cat fight.

Nobody responds.

SUE finishes her cup of coffee and flips it over on the saucer.

SUE: I was just saying I want our daughters to be happy.

SENKA: Something like that, anyway.

EMIR: You want our daughters to be happy, *jel da* [right]?

SUE: *Da.* [Yes.]

EMIR: Is that why you yell at Maja at hospital?

SUE: You know what she want to do is not okay.

EMIR: She can name her son whatever she want. It's not our business.

SUE: Are you mad? She want to call him Abaz!

EMIR: So? Let her.

SUE: You no remember? You have bullet hole in memory or what, Emir?

EMIR: I remember you almost rip off my throat when I said it was beautiful name. I gonna say even more: I adore it!

SUE: He testing me. He gone completely mad! *Allah, pomozi mi.* [Allah, help me.]

EMIR: Why are you so sad, darling?

AGATA: Tata, I don't think you're going to be happy with me.

EMIR: Jewel of my eyes, there is nothing you could do that would upset me.

SUE: Ha! We gonna see about that.

EMIR: Shht, *bolan*! *Pusti nas na miru.* [Leave us alone.] What is it Gata, tell me.

AGATA: Tata . . . I'm in love.

EMIR: Yes! Good news, darling, good news.

AGATA: With a woman.

EMIR: Well . . . Is there something you want to say, Suzo? This gonna be my fault, too? Two out of three of our daughters don't want men because of me?

SUE: I not gonna to say that, Emir.

EMIR: Pfft! Please. I know you. If it doesn't come out now, it gonna come tomorrow. Get the venom out, while it still fresh.

SUE: I no snake, Emir.

EMIR: Could have fooled me.

SUE: So what, you okay with this?

EMIR: This not okay. You want to travel? We send you to Bosnia to find real man. A good Muslim man like Ahmet Ahmetić!

SENKA: Arg! Can we please leave Ahmet out of this?

EMIR: Why leave out a man who barely around, hah? You go to visit Sarajevo last summer and find yourself a double A: Ahmet Ahmetić. This man A++ personality, no? Rich, good looking, smart enough to ask Canadian woman to marry him. Now he visiting Canada once a month, getting to know the real estate! Ha! Good businessman! Fertilizing the soil before taking possession of his private property!

SENKA: Ugh! Unbelievable! I am not his possession or anyone's private property!

SUE: *(to JIDU)* My daughter gonna give him Canadian citizenship—the Bosnian dream!

SENKA: For the last time: Ahmet doesn't care about Canada! He comes here for me. For you! To connect with *us*!

EMIR: Of course, honey—we know that. He care about you. That's why I say to Agata, go to Sarajevo, maybe Ahmet have a cousin looking to marry beautiful Canadian woman.

SENKA: This is too much!

AGATA: Tata . . .

EMIR: No, Tata! You never gonna be allowed to marry woman, period. I no care what the law say in Canada.

AGATA and SENKA are numb. Their ribs fold, their shoulders drop.

JIDU: Emir, I know we haven't seen each other in almost a decade. You were like a father figure to me when I was growing up—

EMIR: Speak, Jidu—don't beat around bush like girl.

JIDU: I hate it when you do that.

EMIR: Do what?

JIDU: Call me a girl.

EMIR: You look like a man now, but you must act like one.

JIDU: I am! I'm saying you're a lucky man. I wish I had a family like you.

EMIR: You no ever gonna have family, Jidu! You thirty something and still in love with Maja.

SENKA: Oh, Tata—

AGATA: Jidu's our friend.

JIDU: Please—I got this. *(beat)* Man, Emir. You really don't give a shit about anyone's feelings, do you?

EMIR: Real man see what going on, Jidu. You hopelessly in love with my daughter. And she prefer sperm bank from America, pah!

SUE: *Bože dragi!* [Dear God!] Emir!

JIDU: That's fine, it's Maja's choice. But even if there was a chance, Emir, I know you would never consent to your daughter being with a Brown man like me.

JIDU starts for the door.

EMIR: You think I racist or what? If my daughter say she love a man, I don't stand in her way no matter what! My daughter here gonna marry a man we barely know! Maybe if your name Jidu Jidić, you have better luck with my daughters! Ha!

JIDU: Sure, Maja may not want me now. She may never want me. And you know why? Do you remember Sarajevo? *(beat)* She blames herself for it. She's scared, Emir. And she's suffering alone. Always alone! She thinks that if she cares too much about somebody, she'll lose them too. Her brain won't let her love me no matter what her heart feels. So I wait. I'm there for her. I travel across the country just to hold her. And like an idiot, I've held onto the hope that one day, she'll let me in. *(beat)* I know I'm a fool. You all know I'm in love with her! She chose a sperm donor over me and I still care about her. That's the difference between a man like me and a man like you, Emir. I don't stop caring just because I'm not getting what I want. And that's it!

JIDU exits, slamming the door.

EMIR: What happen? Why I fight with Jidu, hah? *(continues to pace around)* I no remember why I so mad at him! *Ma šta mi se dešava?* [What's happening to me?] My whole life turn upside down!

SUE: Emir, *slušaj me* [listen to me]. You mad, *ljubavi.* You need relax and breathe.

EMIR: I know. I scared, Suzo. I losing my mind.

SUE: You have no time to be scare right now. You must to go get Jidu before he leaves.

EMIR: Ah, no, impossible! You must to go get him. Tell him I gone crazy. He gonna understand, it's Jidu.

SUE: Oh, no, Emir. You not gonna get away with this one. Go get Jidu right now, I say. That's it!

EMIR: Fine, but maybe he gone already.

SENKA: With that snowstorm? He's probably still heating up the car.

EMIR exits as MAJA enters on stage wearing pyjamas and slippers.

MAJA: What on earth is going on?

AGATA: Don't ask.

MAJA: Where's Jidu?

SENKA's phone rings.

SUE: Answer! It's Ahmet!

SENKA: Ahi? *(beat)* Oh, my God, it's so nice to hear your voice. *(beat)* I'm okay. Are you okay? *(beat)* Okay, good.

SUE: What going on?

SENKA: They let him go. *(beat)* All flights to Ottawa have been cancelled cuz of the snowstorm. He's going to stay there overnight and take a flight tomorrow. *(beat)* Did they treat you okay? *(beat)* Good, that's good! *(beat)* Oh, us? Well—we celebrated Gata's birthday. *(beat)* It's okay, don't worry. They understand, obviously. *(beat)* It was, yeah—it was *(beat)* good. She—we—it's a long story. Tell you later. *(beat)* Okay. Good. I'll see you in the morning. *Volim te, ljubavi* [I love you]. Good night.

AGATA: I'm happy everything's okay.

SENKA: They just detained him for nothing! Because they could. Can you believe it?

SUE: Well, that's good news. Tide is changing.

MAJA: Is it?

EMIR and JIDU enter.

SENKA: I'm sorry, Jidu.

JIDU: It's okay, I lost control. I'm sorry too. It's been a stressful evening *(laughs)*.

AGATA: Tell me about it.

SUE: It's over now. Ahmet called. They let him go. Good omen.

JIDU: That's good news.

MAJA: Are you okay?

JIDU nods. Their hands touch very briefly.

Meanwhile, EMIR walks to the couch.

If possible: he hits the lamp but doesn't react.

SENKA: All wonderful news, if you think about it. Maja's pregnant. Agata finally told the parents she's a lesbian.

MAJA: What?

AGATA: Yeah . . .

SUE: *(look of horror)* Don't call my child that word, please!

MAJA hugs and kisses AGATA.

SENKA: Lesbian's not a bad word. It's a simple fact: Agata is an Amazon, a lesbian, queer, whatever word she wants to use is just fine.

MAJA: Freud says we're all born bisexuals.

SUE: You no right, Senka. And you, Maja—

JIDU: Let's not start again! I'm at my limit, for real.

SUE: Tonight is going to get better, I can feel it. *(beat)* Look at that, I forgot to read the coffee cup!

SUE turns the cup.

Hmm . . .

EMIR: What is it, Suzo?

SENKA: What do you see?

SUE: It not what you see, but how you look.

EMIR: Come on, *ženo*. Tell us!

SUE: It's Maja's baby.

MAJA: What?

SUE: He . . . he not gonna be positioned right.

SENKA: Ah, breech position?

AGATA: That's no big deal, is it?

MAJA: I don't know.

EMIR: She can get a Caesarean, like you.

SUE: Yes . . . you remember?

EMIR: You had Maja like that.

MAJA: Nope, not me.

SENKA: It wasn't me.

AGATA: Nor me.

Brief pause.

SUE: You remember, Emi? *(beat)* Abaz?

The silence betrays the iron taste of war.

SUE's eyes scream: my baby! I've lost my flesh and blood!

Reci mi da ga se sjećaš! Kako možeš zaboraviti? Nije me briga ako imaš oštećeni mozak, Emir, nemaš pravo da ga zaboraviš! [Tell me you remember him. How could you forget? I don't care if you have a broken brain, Emir, you don't have the right to forget him.]

SENKA: Forget who? Who's Abaz?

SUE: *Znam da znaš o čemu pričam.* [I know you know what I'm talking about.]

EMIR: Oh *(beat) da, sjećam se.* [Yes, I remember.]

EMIR experiences a PTSD flashback; he finally remembers.

Suggestion: sound of bombs, like in MAJA's last flashback.

AGATA: What's going on, Tata? Mama?

SENKA: He's hallucinating.

SUE: No. He *remembering.*

EMIR: *(as if in a trance) Hajde, idi se igrati ali pazi.* [Go play but be careful.]

JIDU: What did he just say?

SENKA: "Go play but be careful." *(to EMIR)* Who were you talking to, Tata?

EMIR: *Ja sam kriv.* [It's my fault.]

Suggestion: sudden, deadly sound of a sniper.

EMIR falls to his knees.

MAJA: Tata!

JIDU: Emir!

AGATA: Oh, God.

EMIR: How I could have forgotten?

SUE: *Kako se usuđuješ zaboraviti? Ha? Kako si ga mogao pustiti iz vida?* [How dare you forget? How could you have let him out of your sight?]

EMIR: *Oprosti mi, Suzo. Sve se dogodilo tako brzo. Voleo bih da sam ja umro.* [Forgive me, Sue. It all happened so quickly. I wish it had been me who'd died.]

SUE: *Moj jedini sin . . .* [My only son . . .]

EMIR: *I moj sin.* [My son, too.]

MAJA: Abaz . . .

AGATA: Abaz?

SENKA: We have a brother?

MAJA: Had.

SUE: *Mjesec dana prije nego što smo pobjegli iz opsjednutog Sarajeva, izgubila sam svojeg sina! Taj dan—nikada neću zaboraviti.* [A month before we escaped the siege of Sarajevo, I lost my child. That day—I'll never forget it.]

Brief pause.

Nemaš mi ništa za reći? Emir! Pričamo o Abazu! [You have nothing to say to me? Emir! We're talking about Abaz!]

EMIR: *Žao mi je . . . Ne znam šta da kažem.* [I'm sorry . . . I don't know what to say.]

SUE: *Uvijek ista priča, ne znam zašto išta očekujem od tebe.* [Always the same story, I don't know why I expect anything of you.]

MAJA: Mama . . .

EMIR: *Oprosti mi.* [Forgive me.]

SUE: I wear this sweater last time Abaz hug me. His little face . . . his little hands. Some days I wake up and I wonder, how they could be dead? *Ljubav mamina.* [My love.]

Brief pause.

EMIR painfully pulls out words from hidden depths.

EMIR: There was no cloud in the sky that day. It was supposed to be ceasefire. I take the children to the market to buy bread. *(beat)* Abi want to play marbles with some boys. *(beat)* I say okay, go for it, but Maja has to come with you. She didn't want to go, but I told her she had to. What an idiot!

MAJA: You couldn't have known what would happen. It's not your fault.

EMIR: It all happen so quickly. Bombs started falling suddenly. Snipers shooting at us. It was chaos. Hell . . .

SUE: *Allah bismilah ira ham ira him, oprosti nam bože.* [Arabic prayer: "In the Name of Allah, Most Gracious Most Merciful." Followed by Bosnian: "Forgive us God."]

EMIR: How could a human being do something like that? I no understand . . .

AGATA: What happened?

SUE: I told you they not allowed to go out! You take them anyway! Only one child come back to me alive!

SUE hits EMIR's chest.

Fool! Brute!

AGATA: Mama!

SUE: *Izgubljen za uvijek*! [He's gone forever!]

EMIR: If only that sniper had shot me. If only I'd been the one to die.

MAJA: Oh, Tata. Please don't say that.

EMIR: I didn't protect him.

MAJA: Neither did I . . . we couldn't do anything.

SUE: Our son is buried with strangers in mass grave. *(beat)* I wanted to go back a million times. But you—you!

EMIR: *I to je moja greška.* [That's also my fault.] I couldn't go back . . . Had to keep moving forward. Keep going or . . . or kill myself.

SUE: Emir—

MAJA: Tata—

SENKA: I'm so sorry.

AGATA: Me too . . .

SUE: Why you not tell me this before?

Beat.

EMIR: I so sorry, Suzo . . .

SUE: You never want to talk about Abi so I do the same. I keep it all here and sometimes it hurting me like a cancer.

EMIR: I see him in your eyes . . . It's like *(beat)* I half-dead, half-alive, can't feel anything. So angry. Can't remember.

SENKA: You suffered in silence . . .

SUE: But pain persist. *(beat)* Most of family photos were destroyed. I have only one of Abaz hidden in my wallet.

SUE gets her bag and takes out the photograph.

Here, look at him, my boy.

AGATA: He kinda looks like me.

SUE: He would have been tall and lean like you.

MAJA: And maybe with the same haircut.

SUE: Always in my heart.

EMIR: How could I forget his name? I'm sorry, *ljubavi.*

SUE: I don't know, Emir. I don't know how to accept your apology.

EMIR: It's my fault Abi dead.

SUE: Well—oh—you not the one who pulled the trigger!

EMIR: I should not let him go.

SUE: And since then, what, Emir? You no allow yourself to live!

EMIR: Honestly, Suzo, living scare me. *(to AGATA)* That's why I no want you to go and travel. *(to SENKA)* You too. I like it better when we all in same place together.

SENKA: You can get help, you know? I have a friend who specializes in trauma. And Maja, God: you probably suffer from survivor's guilt.

JIDU: She knows.

MAJA: Can we do this later, Senka? I'm exhausted.

SUE: *(to EMIR)* You better not forget anymore, you hear me? *(to MAJA)* And you.

MAJA: Mama . . .

SUE: I sorry I make a scene at hospital and humiliate you in front of the doctors, *Majo moja*—I go crazy when you say you gonna call your son Abaz.

MAJA: I'm sorry, too. I shouldn't have dropped it like that in the car. *(sighs)* Mama?

SUE: Yes, *ljubavi*?

MAJA: Are you mad at me?

SUE: Of course, *sine*. I mad at you for abandoning us for eight years. Eight whole years! *Allahu moj!* [My God!]

MAJA: I know. I'm sorry about that. Are you mad about the name?

EMIR: I love the name.

An expectant pause.

Don't worry, I not forget! I know she naming her son after her brother.

MAJA: I should have asked your permission first, Tata.

EMIR: That's true.

MAJA: How do you feel about it?

EMIR: I okay with it. Your mother have final decision here.

SUE: Listen, this is big thing you want to do, Maja. This is affect the whole family, not just you.

MAJA: I'm conscious of that. I think, I guess, I came all the way home to talk through this but it came out all wrong.

SUE: *Ljubavi Majo* [My dear Maja], I gonna need a few days to think of it.

MAJA: I understand.

AGATA: I'm so glad you're home . . .

SENKA: It's true, *Majo*. I'm also happy you're home. I hope we can spend some quality time together.

MAJA: Me too.

SENKA: *Ich habe dich vermisst.* [German: I missed you.]

MAJA: *Ich liebe dich.* [German: I love you.]

SUE: You see? What I tell you? There *is* God after all—

SENKA and MAJA make peace.

EMIR: Sue, listen to me. I know you want to divorce me for twenty years now. I haven't been good husband.

SUE: You no care about me.

EMIR: That's no true, *ljubavi. Volim te, Suzo,* [I love you, Sue] more than anything in the world. Without you and girls, I don't know who or where I gonna be.

Pause.

I sorry I neglect you. You stunning. I love your dress, your hair, your eyes, and all your body.

SUE: *Hajde ba . . .* [Come on . . .]

EMIR: I want to marry you.

SUE: You proposing to me, Emir?

EMIR: Yes—Suzana Bolić, will you be my wife *(beat)* again?

JIDU: All right! A proposal!

MAJA: Oh dear God.

SUE: Yes! Yes, I will! But on one condition.

EMIR: Anything!

SUE: The lamp stay. Painting must go.

EMIR: Of course. We even keep that ugly pink bowl, how about that?

JIDU: Well. Tonight is ending on a much brighter note than I ever expected. *(beat)* I don't want to overstay my welcome. Thank you for having me. Truly.

EMIR: Please, Jidu. You can't go out in that storm.

SENKA: Sleep here.

AGATA: Yes, spend the night. With Maja.

MAJA: Agata!

AGATA: What?

MAJA: How old are you again?

EMIR: Jidu gonna take the basement, right Jidu?

JIDU: Of course, Emir.

SENKA: I wonder how long your second honeymoon will last.

SUE: Honeymoon? That's good idea.

EMIR: We go to Japan. With Agata.

AGATA: Good one, Tata.

SUE: I want to go to Latin America. How about Argentina?

EMIR: Okay. We go to Argentina, just you and me. We gonna have a great time. We gonna eat steak!

SUE: We gonna dance the tango. Go to local theatre.

EMIR: Even better: we go to south of Argentina and see the penguins.

SUE: No, Emir! You promise you gonna be good husband. You take me to fancy restaurant in big city.

MAJA: Mama—

EMIR: We rent Bibi-Air apartment with kitchen, much cheaper. Then, I personally take you shopping with my Mastercard and buy you biggest pot Activia cranberry yogurt in the world.

SUE: You joking Emir, or what?

EMIR: Of course I joking, Suzo. You know I only like Activia plain. *(to JIDU)* It's the best!

AGATA: Tata—

SUE: I want to go to theatre, see big show. I don't care if we don't speak Spanish. I love the way the language sounds—the rhythm, the music.

EMIR: Why you wanna go waste money at theatre, hah? Nobody go to theatre anyways! We go see movie. It's cheaper, *bona*.

SENKA: Oh, God—

SUE: I want to dress up! I want to be part of social experience!

EMIR: Yeah, yeah, okay. I take you see the new action movie I been waiting for—

SUE: That's it! I not going to South America with you to see movie I can see anywhere!

EMIR:	**SUE:**	**AGATA:**	**SENKA:**	**JIDU:**	**MAJA:**
		Tata!	Mama!		Tata!
I take you see action movie—	No way!	Let's all just relax—	Tata, please!	Oh man . . .	Calm down!
What?	Unbeliev-able!	And breathe—	Ugh . . .	Everyone, please—	God . . .
Oh, please!	Emir!		*(sighs)*		
That's it! *(slams table)*	That's it!	That's it!	That's it!	That's it!	That's it! *(holds belly)*

EMIR: End of story!

The End

ACKNOWLEDGMENTS

Blissful State of Surrender is my first play. Written over one intense and inspired weekend, I spent five years developing it with a generous and diverse bunch of collaborators who deserve my thanks. In its early stages of development, the play was dramaturged by Greg Link and received insightful feedback from a handful of readers in Sudbury. It was then picked up by Sarah Garton Stanley as part of the March Mayhem workshop series at the National Arts Centre before spending three years in various in-person and online workshops at TACTICS, an indie theatre development hub based in Ottawa. During the pandemic, I continued to develop the play with the generous support of Artistic Director Eric Coates while a playwright in residence at the Great Canadian Theatre Company (GCTC). Somewhere along the way, I started my own company, Blissful Productions, and in partnership with TACTICS as presenter and GCTC as host, I produced *Blissful State of Surrender* in time for its world premiere on February 22, 2022, at the Great Canadian Theatre Company, just a few days after Ontario made it legal for us to gather again. It would not have been possible to have an in-person run of the play without the leadership of Sarah Kitz, the new artistic director of the GCTC, as well as the theatre's talented and extraordinary team.

I want to extend my sincere gratitude to the many collaborators who brought this story to life. Some were there from the early beginnings, starting with the NAC reading where I met Kate Smith, followed by the TACTICS workshops, which from the start included Dana Užarević, John Koensgen, Danielle Savoie, and Laurie Champagne. Directed by Jan Irwin, the workshops eventually featured the entire cast and early designers including Anurag Choudhury, Andrea Massoud, and Suad Bushnaq. Bronwyn Steinberg, who for years saw through the play's development as Artistic Director of TACTICS, directed the world premiere, leading a large production that included Laurie Shannon, Jennifer Goodman, Vanessa Imeson, Vanessa Lachance, and Arielle Voght. Jamaal Jackson Rogers, our cultural consultant, helped support my treatment of internalized oppression and lateral violence with sensitivity and care. In a play about the impacts of genocide and Islamophobia, holding the balance between showing the victimization of Bosniak people while addressing the privileges of white skin and heteropatriarchy can be, and has been, a double-edged sword.

I am also indebted to collaborators whose post-production insights and support were invaluable, including Keith Barker, Joël Beddows, and Kareem Fahmy. If this long, delightful, and at times painful process of development has taught me anything it's that writing is rewriting and writing is a collaborative act, mantras I picked up from Nadia Bozak while a creative writing student at Carleton University.

I have not been able to write about the impacts of war and genocide without leaning into humour precisely because the horrors and wounds remain too raw, and all too real. *Blissful State of Surrender* opened as war broke out in Ukraine; this book is being published as war crimes, genocides, censorship, and the rise of right-wing populism strengthens its hold around the world; history, regrettably, repeats itself. I am grateful to all the audience members and readers who continue to bear witness to stories that directly confront trauma and loss; as Susan Sontag and Judith Butler suggest, one of the functions of witnessing is to connect with the pain of others, particularly of distant others. Since the ancients, theatre has allowed our hearts to beat in unison as we hold our breaths, laugh, cry, witness, and transform together. While I have written this story from the point of view of Bosniak survivors, it is in honour of all the children and people who have not survived; who are barely surviving; and who thrive despite war and genocide past and present.

Sanita Fejzić is a playwright, poet, and literary writer. *Blissful State of Surrender*, which premiered at the Great Canadian Theatre Company in 2022, was nominated for five Rideau Awards, including for Dana Užarević, who won Best Actress. In 2023, Sanita produced *Why Worry About Their Futures* at the undercurrents festival, a tryptic of three short plays—*The Sky It Falls* by Keith Barker, *The Auden Test* by Lawrence Aronovitch, and her own play *Expecting*. Sanita articulated an artistic movement she calls Peasant Futurisms while completing her PH.D. in cultural studies at Queen's University. Peasant Futurisms expresses peasant perspectives of the future, past, and present through organic subsistence farming, local gift and cyclical economies, and collaborative labour models. The child of Bosniak peasants, Sanita is interested in healing people and the planet through peasant subsistence farming, permaculture gardening, agro-ecology, and organic regenerative agriculture (conservation and rehabilitation approaches to growing food). Her radio play *Machines and Moss*, produced by the National Arts Centre, is part of the Peasant Futurist movement and is presently being adapted into a graphic novel. Her poetry and short fiction have been published in magazines across the country and beyond and she has been shortlisted for the CBC Poetry Prize (2018) and the Malahat Review Long Poem Prize (2019). Her novella, *Psychomachia*, was shortlisted for the

Ken Klonski Novella Prize (2016) and the Canada Relit Awards (2018), and her creative nonfiction was longlisted for the 2019 CBC Nonfiction Prize. Her first collection of poetry, *Refugee Mouth*, is forthcoming from Frontenac Press. Sanita lives with her wife and two children on the traditional unceded territory of the Algonquin Anishinaabeg people in Ottawa, Canada. Originally from Bosnia and Herzegovina, she fled the Siege of Sarajevo and genocide of her Bosniak people at the age of seven and lived as a refugee, illegal immigrant, and "temporary guest" across three countries before seeking permanent refuge in Canada. More at www.sanitafejzic.com.